# THE SECOND
# FOUR BOOKS
# OF POEMS

OTHER BOOKS OF POETRY

BY W.S. MERWIN

---

*A Mask for Janus (1952)*

*The Dancing Bears (1954)*

*Green With Beasts (1956)*

*The Drunk in the Furnace (1960)*

*The Moving Target (1963)*

*The Lice (1967)*

*The Carrier of Ladders (1970)*

*Writings to an Unfinished Accompaniment (1973)*

*The First Four Books of Poems (1975)*
(INCLUDING THE COMPLETE TEXTS OF
*A Mask for Janus, The Dancing Bears,
Green with Beasts* AND *The Drunk in the Furnace)*

*The Compass Flower (1977)*

*Finding the Islands (1982)*

*Opening the Hand (1983)*

*The Rain in the Trees (1988)*

*Selected Poems (1988)*

*Travels (1993)*

# W. S.
# MERWIN

---

# THE SECOND
# FOUR BOOKS
# OF POEMS

---

*The Moving Target*

*The Lice*

*The Carrier of Ladders*

*Writings to an Unfinished Accompaniment*

---

*Copper Canyon Press*

The books collected in this volume were originally published
by Atheneum and edited by Harry Ford:
*The Moving Target*, 1963
*The Lice*, 1967
*The Carrier of Ladders*, 1970
*Writings to an Unfinished Accompaniment*, 1973

Poems in this collection have appeared in *Abraxas; American Poems, A Contemporary
Collection; American Poetry Now; The American Scholar; Antæus; The Atlantic Monthly;
Choice; The Beloit Poetry Journal; The Berkshire Review; Blue Grass; Chelsea; Chicago
Tribune; The Columbia Forum; Contemporary American Verse; Dakotah Review; The
Distinctive Voice; Encounter; Evergreen Review; Field; Harpers Bazaar; Harpers
Magazine; The Hudson Review; The Iowa Review; The Journal of Creative Behavior; Kayak;
Lillabulero; The Listener; The Nation; New American Review; New Directions Annual;
The New Republic; The New York Quarterly; The New York Review of Books; The New
Yorker; The Paris Review; Partisan Review; P.E.N. New Poems 1961; Poems from the Floating
World Vol. 5; Poetry; Poets' Choice; Princeton Library Chronicle; Quarterly Review of Literature;
The San Francisco Review; The Saturday Evening Post; Seneca Review; The Seventies; The
Southern Review; Sumac; The Sydney Bulletin; Tri Quarterly; Trobar.*

Publication of this book is supported by a grant from the National Endowment for the
Arts and a grant from the Lannan Foundation. Additional support to Copper Canyon
Press has been provided by the Andrew W. Mellon Foundation, the Lila Wallace-Reader's
Digest Fund, and the Washington State Arts Commission. Copper Canyon Press is in
residence with Centrum at Fort Worden State Park.

*Library of Congress Cataloging-in-Publication Data*
Merwin, W.S. (William Stanley), 1927–
[Poems. Selections]
The second four books of poems / W.S. Merwin.
p.    cm.
Contents: The moving target—The lice—The carrier of ladders—Writings to an
unfinished accompaniment.
ISBN 1-55659-054-7 : $14.00
I. Title.   II. Title: 2nd 4 books of poems.
PS3563.E75A6   1993
811'.54—dc20   92-39320

COPPER CANYON PRESS
Post Office Box 271
Port Townsend, Washington 98368

# CONTENTS

## ～ *The Moving Target, 1963*

## The Lice, 1967

## *The Carrier of Ladders, 1970*

## *Writings To An Unfinished Accompaniment, 1973*

The title, with its numerological hopscotch, is of course intended to indicate that this book is the sequel to *The First Four Books of Poems,* originally published in 1975, which assembled the volumes of poems that I had written between 1947 and 1958.

The four volumes that make up the present collection span the sixties and the early years of the seventies. In several respects that have been noted since the first of them, *The Moving Target,* was published in 1963, they embody pronounced changes from the poems in the four books that preceded them. From the beginning they are less obviously formal – it might be more to the point to say that whatever may provide their form is less apparent. By the end of the poems in *The Moving Target* I had relinquished punctuation along with several other structural conventions, a move that evolved from my growing sense that punctuation alluded to and assumed an allegiance to the rational protocol of written language, and of prose in particular. I had come to feel that it stapled the poems to the page. Whereas I wanted the poems to evoke the spoken language, and wanted the hearing of them to be essential to taking them in.

By the time *The Lice* appeared in 1967 these formal changes and even some of the changes in tone and content that went with them, seemed less surprising to those who remarked on them in print, and it was possible for the new book to be considered as a reflection of its historic context, the world of the sixties.

It was an era, indeed an age, that has now receded a quarter of a century into the past and has become a time of legend. For many of us who lived through that period it remains in our minds as a moment of remarkable contradictions. There were the creeds of the flower children and the proliferation of nuclear weapons, the up-welling civil rights passions and the assassinations of King and the Kennedys, a nascent ecological consciousness and the development of events that became the undeclared war in Vietnam. Wild aspiration and vertiginous despair existed not alternately but at

once, and at times we may have clung to visionary hopes not so much be-
cause they were really credible as because we felt it would be not only
mean-spirited but fatal to abandon them. We knew a kind of willful des-
peration.

As we remember that time, some of us notice another contradiction,
one that I suppose is familiar to many people in recalling moments of ex-
ceptional intensity. We know that age to be utterly beyond reach now, ir-
retrievably past, a period whose distance we already feel as though it had
stretched into centuries, and yet it appears to us to be not only recent but
present, still with us not as a memory but as a part of our unfinished days, a
ground or backdrop before which we live. It could be said that we are
haunted by it, which would suggest that that time was not done with in us,
that what we saw and felt then is still part of our incompleteness and our
choices.

Of course I hope that is not the only reason why these books may still be
read, and I hope that readers will continue to come to the poems and want
to keep them long after the circumstances of the sixties and of the present
century have gone. If they do so it will be because such readers continue to
share with us something of history that is not strictly historic, something
because of which we continue to write and read but which our words can
never finally name.

Poems are written in moments of history, and their circumstances bear
upon their language and tone and subject and feeling whether the authors
are conscious of that happening or not, but it is hard to conceive of a poem
being written only out of historic occasion. Somebody who was not a
product of history alone had to be there and feel the need for words, hear
them, summon them together.

My own life in the sixties also seemed to be made of contradictions: City
life and rural life; Europe and America; Love of the old and a craving for
change; Public issues and a disposition to live quietly. What has come to be
called the cost of living was more moderate then. My own tastes were
simple and I managed to live on little. Independence was something I trea-
sured. In the early sixties I had an apartment in New York on the lower
East Side, east of Tompkins Square, on the top floor of a building on East
6th Street that has since been torn down. The rent was very low. The front
rooms looked out over a school and the old roofscapes of lower Manhattan
to the Brooklyn Bridge. A political club, source of sinister rumors, occu-
pied the ground floor of the building next door. Scaffolding came and

went along the sidewalk, rising from the tide-lines of broken glass. Sometimes taxi drivers asked guests whether they really wanted to come to that neighborhood, and occasionally they even refused to drive there, but I loved living there and I walked endlessly through that section of the city and along the river to the end of the island. Much of the latter part of *The Moving Target* and the first part of *The Lice* was written there.

I had been born in New York, in a building that later became part of Columbia University and then was torn down, but I had grown up in other places. I felt bound to that city and time by ties that I was trying to fathom, and the poems reflected something of that and perhaps some of its excitement. They also testified to the deep foreboding that shadowed those years and which has not gone away since.

It was still possible then to take a boat to Europe, and if you applied early enough, even have a cabin to yourself for a couple of hundred dollars. In the early sixties my heaviest expense was travelling back and forth across the Atlantic to spend part of the spring, all summer, and the early fall, in the remote farmhouse in southwest France that I had acquired as a ruin some years before. I could live in that beautiful country for even less money than on the lower East Side. My life there was different in almost every respect from the life I knew in New York, but I had rapidly come to love that region and my neighbors, and to feel deeply attached to what I found there.

I had participated in the movement for nuclear disarmament since the late fifties and the Aldermaston marches in England, and after the Cuban missile crisis I found myself with new and urgent questions. It seemed clearer to me than ever that the menace of military destruction and the accelerating devastation of what remained of the natural world were effects of the same impulse. But one morning, looking south over the roofs of the city that I thought of as my own, I realized that if I were to be asked at that moment what I thought would be a good life I would not have a clear answer or one that would convince me. It occurred to me that I knew next to nothing about things that I took for granted every day: the roof over my head, the things I wore, the food I ate. I was over thirty and I thought it was time to know more about them than I did. Even so, such considerations might have led to nothing more than restless doubt if it had not been for the image of that old farmhouse and the perspectives it suggested. In the spring of 1963 I left New York and spent the next years in France, in the country, and the later poems in *The Lice,* with few exceptions, were written there, as were many of the poems in the two books that followed.

It was not a time or a life exempt from history. Papers, magazines, letters, brought the news. The Vietnam War phase by phase, and the disclosures of cruelty, ruin, arrogance and compounded dishonesty that it produced. The insistent awareness of the human wastage of the rest of life was set against a daily existence, and friendships, sights, sounds, the associations of a place that I regarded as a scarcely credible good fortune. I was convinced that the momentum of human projects was on a very unpromising course, and neither the quiet of the uplands nor the tenor of the news encouraged me to feel that the mere addition of a few more pages to the swelling flow of printed paper was a matter of great importance, but I continued to earn part of my income by translating. I felt at once a profound attraction to the ancient rural world in which I was living and a disquieting recognition of the fragility and uncertainty of my relation to it. For a while I wrote little unless words overtook me in the middle of doing something else such as repairing walls or working in the garden. Some of the latter poems in *The Lice* I wrote at a time when I thought I was not writing at all.

It is scarcely surprising that *The Lice* in particular has been described as dark and pessimistic. The general characterization ignores certain poems but it is true that the book is not predominantly sunny. Subsequent volumes, according to some readers, are less imbued with the imminence of menace and loss, more given to representation of the benison of Life. And so I have been asked whether my notion of our moment and its outlook has become more sanguine. The question, and perhaps these afterthoughts themselves, suggest that these poems were the more or less deliberate outcome of a kind of world-view or private ideology. I began with a resolution never to be guilty of anything of the kind, but poetry like speech itself is made out of paradox, contradiction, irresolvables. It employs words that are general and belong to everybody to convey something, whatever it is, that is specific and unique. It uses comparison to speak of what cannot be compared. It cannot be conscripted even into the service of good intentions. Its sources, as we know, are in sensibilities and the senses, not in reasons and opinions. Yet reasons, thought, opinion, knowledge, contribute to the formation of a sensibility and to the life of the senses. Poets have been known to be smug about their fine uselessness, but the Vietnam War led many poets of my generation to try to use poetry to make something stop happening. We will never know whether all that we wrote shortened that nightmare by one hour, saved a single life or the leaves on one tree, but it seemed unthinkable to many of us not to make the attempt and not to use whatever talent we had in order to do it. In the process we produced a great many bad poems, but our opposition to that horror and degradation was more than an intellectual formulation, and sometimes it tapped depths of bewilderment, grief, rage, admiration, that took us by surprise. Occasionally it called forth writings that may be poems after all.

In the autumn of 1970 I travelled to southern Mexico, to Chiapas, to San Cristóbal de Las Casas, and I spent the winters there until 1973. Many of the poems in *Writings to an Unfinished Accompaniment* were written in an old adobe house on a back street in San Cristóbal – a place and time that added immeasurably to my sense of what has come to be called the Americas.

The current of the news since the most recent of these books was published has done nothing to brighten my view of history and where it is leading. Quite the contrary, perhaps, as cruelty, polymorphous nihilism, and organized obliteration have accelerated, and with them the racing disintegration of the entire evolutionary structure in which we are privileged still to exist. I think it is essential to recognize the probable result of what we have done and are doing, but when we have seen that and its roots in human motives, the menaced world may seem more to be treasured than ever. Certainly the anguish and anger we feel at the threat to it and the sleepless despoiling of it can lose their tragic complexity and become mere bitterness when we forget that their origin is a passion for the momentary countenance of the unrepeatable world.

W.S.M.

# THE

# MOVING

# TARGET

(1963)

## HOME FOR THANKSGIVING

I bring myself back from the streets that open like long
Silent laughs, and the others
Spilled into in the way of rivers breaking up, littered with words,
Crossed by cats and that sort of thing,
From the knowing wires and the aimed windows,
Well this is nice, on the third floor, in back of the billboard
Which says Now Improved and I know what they mean,
I thread my way in and I sew myself in like money.

Well this is nice with my shoes moored by the bed
And the lights around the billboard ticking on and off like a beacon,
I have brought myself back like many another crusty
Unbarbered vessel launched with a bottle,
From the bare regions of pure hope where
For a great part of the year it scarcely sets at all,
And from the night skies regularly filled with old movies of my fingers,
Weightless as shadows, groping in the sluices,
And from the visions of veins like arteries, and
From the months of plying
Between can and can, vacant as a pint in the morning,
While my sex grew into the only tree, a joyless evergreen,
And the winds played hell with it at night, coming as they did
Over at least one thousand miles of emptiness,
Thumping as though there were nothing but doors, insisting
"Come out," and of course I would have frozen.

Sunday, a fine day, with my ears wiped and my collar buttoned
I went for a jaunt all the way out and back on
A streetcar and under my hat with the dent settled
In the right place I was thinking maybe — a thought
Which I have noticed many times like a bold rat —
I should have stayed making some of those good women
Happy, for a while at least, Vera with
The eau-de-cologne and the small fat dog named Joy,
Gladys with her earrings, cooking and watery arms, the one

With the limp and the fancy sheets, some of them
Are still there I suppose, oh no,

I bring myself back avoiding in silence
Like a ship in a bottle.
I bring my bottle.
Or there was thin Pearl with the invisible hair nets, the wind would not
Have been right for them, they would have had
Their times, rugs, troubles,
They would have wanted curtains, cleanings, answers, they would have
Produced families their own and our own, hen friends and
Other considerations, my fingers sifting
The dark would have turned up other
Poverties, I bring myself
Back like a mother cat transferring her only kitten,
Telling myself secrets through my moustache,
They would have wanted to drink ship, sea, and all or
To break the bottle, well this is nice,
Oh misery, misery, misery,
You fit me from head to foot like a good grade suit of longies
Which I have worn for years and never want to take off.
I did the right thing after all.


A LETTER FROM GUSSIE


If our father were alive
The stains would not be defiling
The walls, nor the splintery porch
Be supported mostly by ants,
The garden, gone to the bad,
(Though that was purely Mother's)
Would not have poked through the broken
Window like an arm,
And you would never have dared

Behave toward me in this manner,
Like no gentleman and no brother,
Not even a card at Christmas
Last Christmas, and once again
Where are my dividends?

This is my reward
For remaining with our mother
Who always took your part,
You and your investments
With what she made me give you.
Don't you think I'd have liked
To get away also?
I had the brochures ready
And some nice things that fitted.
After all it isn't as though
You'd ever married. Oh
And the plumbing if I may say so
Would not have just lain down,
And the school children
Would not keep drilling the teeth
Which I no longer have
With their voices, and each time
I go out with a mouthful of clothespins
The pits of the hoodlums would not be
Dug nearer to the back steps.
Maybe you think my patience
Endures forever, maybe
You think I will die. The goat
If you recall I mentioned
I had for a while, died.
And Mother's canary, I
Won't pretend I was sorry.
Maybe you want me to think
You've died yourself, but I have
My information. I've told
Some people of consequence,

So anything can happen.
Don't say I didn't warn you.
I've looked long enough on the bright side,
And now I'm telling you
I won't stir from Mother's chair
Until I get an answer.
Morning noon and night
Can come and go as they please,
And the man from the funeral parlor
To change the calendars,
But I won't go to bed at all
Unless they come and make me,
And they'll have to bend me flat
Before they can put me away.


## LEMUEL'S BLESSING

*Let Lemuel bless with the wolf, which is a
dog without a master, but the Lord hears his
cries and feeds him in the desert.*
    CHRISTOPHER SMART: *Jubilate Agno*

You that know the way,
Spirit,
I bless your ears which are like cypresses on a mountain
With their roots in wisdom. Let me approach.
I bless your paws and their twenty nails which tell their own prayer
And are like dice in command of their own combinations.
Let me not be lost.
I bless your eyes for which I know no comparison.
Run with me like the horizon, for without you
I am nothing but a dog lost and hungry,
Ill-natured, untrustworthy, useless.

My bones together bless you like an orchestra of flutes.
Divert the weapons of the settlements and lead their dogs a dance.
Where a dog is shameless and wears servility

In his tail like a banner,
Let me wear the opprobrium of possessed and possessors
As a thick tail properly used
To warm my worst and my best parts. My tail and my laugh bless you.
Lead me past the error at the fork of hesitation.
Deliver me

From the ruth of the lair, which clings to me in the morning,
Painful when I move, like a trap;
Even debris has its favorite positions but they are not yours;
From the ruth of kindness, with its licked hands;
I have sniffed baited fingers and followed
Toward necessities which were not my own: it would make me
An habitué of back steps, faithful custodian of fat sheep;

From the ruth of prepared comforts, with its
Habitual dishes sporting my name and its collars and leashes of vanity;

From the ruth of approval, with its nets, kennels, and taxidermists;
It would use my guts for its own rackets and instruments, to play its
    own games and music;
Teach me to recognize its platforms, which are constructed like
    scaffolds;

From the ruth of known paths, which would use my feet, tail, and ears
    as curios,
My head as a nest for tame ants,
My fate as a warning.

I have hidden at wrong times for wrong reasons.
I have been brought to bay. More than once.
Another time, if I need it,
Create a little wind like a cold finger between my shoulders, then
Let my nails pour out a torrent of aces like grain from a threshing
    machine;
Let fatigue, weather, habitation, the old bones, finally,

Be nothing to me,
Let all lights but yours be nothing to me.
Let the memory of tongues not unnerve me so that I stumble or quake.

But lead me at times beside the still waters;
There when I crouch to drink let me catch a glimpse of your image
Before it is obscured with my own.

Preserve my eyes, which are irreplaceable.
Preserve my heart, veins, bones,
Against the slow death building in them like hornets until the place is
　　entirely theirs.
Preserve my tongue and I will bless you again and again.

Let my ignorance and my failings
Remain far behind me like tracks made in a wet season,
At the end of which I have vanished,
So that those who track me for their own twisted ends
May be rewarded only with ignorance and failings.
But let me leave my cry stretched out behind me like a road
On which I have followed you.
And sustain me for my time in the desert
On what is essential to me.


BY DAY AND BY NIGHT


Shadow, index of the sun,
Who knows him as you know him,
Who have never turned to look at him since the beginning?

In the court of his brilliance
You set up his absence like a camp.
And his fire only confirms you. And his death is your freedom.

## IN THE GORGE

Lord of the bow,
Our jagged hands
Like the ends of a broken bridge
Grope for each other in silence
Over the loose water.
Have you left us nothing but your blindness?

## SEPARATION

Your absence has gone through me
Like thread through a needle.
Everything I do is stitched with its color.

## THE DEFEATED

Beyond surprise, my ribs start up from the ground.
After I had sunk, the waters went down.
The horizon I was making for runs through my eyes.
It has woven its simple nest among my bones.

## NOAH'S RAVEN

Why should I have returned?
My knowledge would not fit into theirs.
I found untouched the desert of the unknown,
Big enough for my feet. It is my home.
It is always beyond them. The future
Splits the present with the echo of my voice.
Hoarse with fulfilment, I never made promises.


## AS BY WATER

Oh
Together
Embracing departure
We hoisted our love like a sail

And like a sail and its reflection
However
We move and wherever
We shall be divided as by water
Forever forever
Though
Both sails shudder as they go
And both prows lengthen the same sorrow

Till the other elements
Extend between us also.

# THINGS

Possessor
At the approach of winter we are there.
Better than friends, in your sorrows we take no pleasure,
We have none of our own and no memory but yours.
We are the anchor of your future.
Patient as a border of beggars, each hand holding out its whole treasure,

We will be all the points on your compass.
We will give you interest on yourself as you deposit yourself with us.
Be a gentleman: you acquired us when you needed us,
We do what we can to please, we have some beauty, we are helpless,
Depend on us.

# SAVONAROLA

Unable to endure my world and calling the failure God, I will destroy
     yours.

# INSCRIPTION FOR A BURNED BRIDGE

Not your defeats, no.
I have gone in with the river.
I will serve you no longer but you may follow me.

## ECONOMY

No need to break the mirror.
Here is the face shattered,
Good for seven years of sorrow.

## LOST MONTH

The light of the eyes in the house of the crow. Here the gods' voices break and some will never sing again, but some come closer and whisper. Never their names.

There are no hinges. One side of a door is simply forgotten in the other.

In the windows the permissions appear, already lit, unasked, but the wind is the wind of parsimony, and the shadows, which are numerous and large, strain at their slender leashes. One fine day the first knives come through the mirrors, like fins of sharks. The images heal, but imperfectly.

We discover parts of ourselves which came to exist under this influential sign.

## DEAD HAND

Temptations still nest in it like basilisks.
Hang it up till the rings fall.

## ACCLIMATIZATION

I entered at the top of my voice. I forget the song.
It came over me that they were deaf. They gave me
Their praise and left me mute.

I proceeded among them
Like a tourist liner among coin-divers.
I flung them what I had with me. Only then
I saw that their smiles were made of gold, and their
Hands and their wives. They gave me
Their thanks and left me penniless.

It was my fault, I
Got hungry, they fed me. I gave them
My solemn word in payment. And all
The bells in the city rang in triumph
Like cash registers. They gave me their credit
And left me with little hope.
When I woke I discovered
That they had taken my legs leaving me the shoes.

(Oh priceless city, the buildings
Rising at dawn to grip the first light
Like bars, and the mornings shattered
With trees into all the shapes of heartbreak!)

I sit among them
Smiling, but they
Demand, they demand, they demand.
There is no putting them off.
Theirs is the empire, and beyond the empire
There is only ignorance, where I could not survive
Without feet.
To deceive them is to perish. What
Do I have that is my own? I offer my

Degradation as a blind beggar offers his palm.
And I am given
This glass eye to set in the place of tears.


## THE SAINT OF THE UPLANDS

*for Margot Pitt-Rivers*

Their prayers still swarm on me like lost bees.
I have no sweetness. I am dust
Twice over.
          In the high barrens
The light loved us.
Their faces were hard crusts like their farms
And the eyes empty, where vision
Might not come otherwise
Than as water.

They were born to stones; I gave them
Nothing but what was theirs.
I taught them to gather the dew of their nights
Into mirrors. I hung them
Between heavens.

I took a single twig from the tree of my ignorance
And divined the living streams under
Their very houses. I showed them
The same tree growing in their dooryards.
You have ignorance of your own, I said.
They have ignorance of their own.

Over my feet they waste their few tears.

I taught them nothing.
Everywhere
The eyes are returning under the stones. And over
My dry bones they build their churches, like wells.

## THE NAILS

I gave you sorrow to hang on your wall
Like a calendar in one color.
I wear a torn place on my sleeve.
It isn't as simple as that.

Between no place of mine and no place of yours
You'd have thought I'd know the way by now
Just from thinking it over.
Oh I know
I've no excuse to be stuck here turning
Like a mirror on a string,
Except it's hardly credible how
It all keeps changing.
Loss has a wider choice of directions
Than the other thing.

As if I had a system
I shuffle among the lies
Turning them over, if only
I could be sure what I'd lost.
I uncover my footprints, I
Poke them till the eyes open.
They don't recall what it looked like.
When was I using it last?
Was it like a ring or a light
Or the autumn pond
Which chokes and glitters but
Grows colder?
It could be all in the mind. Anyway
Nothing seems to bring it back to me.

And I've been to see
Your hands as trees borne away on a flood,
The same film over and over,

And an old one at that, shattering its account
To the last of the digits, and nothing
And the blank end.

The lightning has shown me the scars of the future.

I've had a long look at someone
Alone like a key in a lock
Without what it takes to turn.

It isn't as simple as that.

Winter will think back to your lit harvest
For which there is no help, and the seed
Of eloquence will open its wings
When you are gone.
But at this moment
When the nails are kissing the fingers good-bye
And my only
Chance is bleeding from me,
When my one chance is bleeding,
For speaking either truth or comfort
I have no more tongue than a wound.


SIRE


Here comes the shadow not looking where it is going,
And the whole night will fall; it is time.
Here comes the little wind which the hour
Drags with it everywhere like an empty wagon through leaves.
Here comes my ignorance shuffling after them
Asking them what they are doing.

Standing still, I can hear my footsteps
Come up behind me and go on

Ahead of me and come up behind me and
With different keys clinking in the pockets,
And still I do not move. Here comes
The white-haired thistle seed stumbling past through the branches
Like a paper lantern carried by a blind man.
I believe it is the lost wisdom of my grandfather
Whose ways were his own and who died before I could ask.

Forerunner, I would like to say, silent pilot,
Little dry death, future,
Your indirections are as strange to me
As my own. I know so little that anything
You might tell me would be a revelation.

Sir, I would like to say,
It is hard to think of the good woman
Presenting you with children, like cakes,
Granting you the eye of her needle,
Standing in doorways, flinging after you
Little endearments, like rocks, or her silence
Like a whole Sunday of bells. Instead, tell me:
Which of my many incomprehensions
Did you bequeath me, and where did they take you? Standing
In the shoes of indecision, I hear them
Come up behind me and go on ahead of me
Wearing boots, on crutches, barefoot, they could never
Get together on any door-sill or destination –
The one with the assortment of smiles, the one
Jailed in himself like a forest, the one who comes
Back at evening drunk with despair and turns
Into the wrong night as though he owned it – oh small
Deaf disappearance in the dusk, in which of their shoes
Will I find myself tomorrow?

## FINALLY

My dread, my ignorance, my
Self, it is time. Your imminence
Prowls the palms of my hands like sweat.
Do not now, if I rise to welcome you,
Make off like roads into the deep night.
The dogs are dead at last, the locks toothless,
The habits out of reach.
I will not be false to you tonight.

Come, no longer unthinkable. Let us share
Understanding like a family name. Bring
Integrity as a gift, something
Which I had lost, which you found on the way.
I will lay it beside us, the old knife,
While we reach our conclusions.

Come. As a man who hears a sound at the gate
Opens the window and puts out the light
The better to see our into the dark,
Look, I put it out.

## THE SHIPS ARE MADE READY IN SILENCE

Moored to the same ring:
The hour, the darkness and I,
Our compasses hooded like falcons.

Now the memory of you comes aching in
With a wash of broken bits which never left port,
In which once we planned voyages.
They come knocking like hearts asking:
What departures on this tide?

Breath of land, warm breath,
You tighten the cold around the navel,
Though all shores but the first have been foreign,
And the first was not home until left behind.

Our choice is ours but we have not made it,
Containing as it does, our destination
Circled with loss as with coral, and
A destination only until attained.

I have left you my hope to remember me by,
Though now there is little resemblance.
At this moment I could believe in no change,
The mast perpetually
Vacillating between the same constellations,
The night never withdrawing its dark virtue
From the harbor shaped as a heart,
The sea pulsing as a heart,
The sky vaulted as a heart,
Where I know the light will shatter like a cry
Above a discovery:
"Emptiness.
Emptiness! Look!"
Look. This is the morning.


ROUTE  WITH  NO  NUMBER


If you want to come after me for any reason
I have left money in the bread-box,
Heart in the ice-box,
And in the mail-box, around the key,
A handkerchief for good-byes.

When you come to the end of the avenue of promises
And the dead bird falls from the limb
Turn away. It is the far fork. When you
Reach the street of the burying beetles
Follow their music as far as it will take you, skirting
The park where the famous
Sleep on their secrets.
And where the shout of the statue has filled
The square with long-dead silence,
Left.
At the turnstile of the hesitants I have left
A ticket for you in a little bee hole at eye level.
The toll keeper is not honest but he is
Cowardly and he has no legs.
Then in the empty boulevard with its view
Of the revolving hills you will see no car-tracks
But you will hear the sound of a streetcar and discover
That the road is moving under your feet, it is
Not bad: rows of portraits on either side
Like cell windows along a corridor, and
Your shadow ducking its head as it passes.

Oh it's passable, and besides I contrive
As I always did, to keep thinking
Of improvements, for instance
The other day ducks went over on their creaking wings
So I thought, "In the future there will be
No more migration, only travel,
No more exile, only distances."
Also it's hard to convey how indifferent
I had become to the jabber of bells
And the senseless applause of clocks.
And then today, without warning, at a place
Where they speak no language, the collectors come through
For my back taxes my present taxes
And my future taxes whether I arrive or not.
I fooled them of course in the old way.
And they fooled me in the old way

And took everything but a few false decisions in the old way,
And I pray for them in the old way:
May the tracks be laid over them
And their fingers be picked off like daisy petals:
"She loathes me, she loathes me not."

Either way, I must tell you, in my present place
I can't hold out hope or any other flags.
There's not even a little privacy: you can see
Eyes lined up to ripen on all the sills.
And once here you're better than I am
If you can find your way back again.
However, I have visited the Day of the Dog,
But it was not yet open and I passed on.
Tell Mrs. H. just the same,
Who said I'd never get anywhere.
What a juncture.
I have gone faithfully into all the churches
And passed on, disappointed.
I have seen streets where the hands of the beggars
Are left out at night like shoes in a hotel corridor.
Several I thought had once been mine and might be again.
I have found many lost things and I have left them that way,
I have created enough disturbance.
I have come on many wasted things.
I have not yet come to my youth.

Now I am sitting
Behind filthy nightscapes, in the echoing room provided,
Among a few retired ornaments.
All the words have been emptied from the books.
The heating is hopeless at any hour. I am
Eating one of my last apples and waiting
For my departure to overtake me
With its empty windows coming up
Like cards, the game
Always turns out the same,
Mother, Father, Luke and John,

My line, my sign, my love,
Think of the cards that were held out to me
And I had to choose this one!


## TO MY BROTHER HANSON

B. *Jan. 28, 1926* / D. *Jan. 28, 1926*

My elder,
Born into death like a message into a bottle,
The tide
Keeps coming in empty on the only shore.
Maybe it has lovers but it has few friends.
It is never still but it keeps its counsel, and

If I address you whose curious stars
Climbed to the tops of their houses and froze,
It is in hope of no
Answer, but as so often, merely
For want of another, for
I have seen catastrophe taking root in the mirror,
And why waste my words there?

Yes, now the roads themselves are shattered
As though they had fallen from a height, and the sky
Is cracked like varnish. Hard to believe,
Our family tree
Seems to be making its mark everywhere.
I carry my head high
On a pike that shall be nameless.

Even so, we had to give up honor entirely,
But I do what I can. I am patient
With the woes of the cupboards, and God knows –
I keep the good word close to hand like a ticket.
I feed the wounded lights in their cages.
I wake up at night on the penultimate stroke, and with

My eyes still shut I remember to turn the thorn
In the breast of the bird of darkness.
I listen to the painful song
Dropping away into sleep.

                    Blood
Is supposed to be thicker. You were supposed to be there
When the habits closed in pushing
Their smiles in front of them, when I was filled
With something else, like a thermometer,
When the moment of departure, standing
On one leg, like a sleeping stork, by the doorway,
Put down the other foot and opened its eye.
I
Got away this time for a while. I've come
Again to the whetted edge of myself where I
Can hear the hollow waves breaking like
Bottles in the dark. What about it? Listen, I've

Had enough of this. Is there nobody
Else in the family
To take care of the tree, to nurse the mirror,
To fix up a bite for hope when the old thing
Comes to the door,
To say to the pans of the balance
Rise up and walk?

## IN THE NIGHT FIELDS

I heard the sparrows shouting "Eat, eat,"
And then the day dragged its carcass in back of the hill.
Slowly the tracks darkened.

The smoke rose steadily from no fires.
The old hunger, left in the old darkness,

Turned like a hanged knife.
I would have preferred a quiet life.
The bugs of regret began their services
Using my spine as a rosary. I left the maps
For the spiders.
Let's go, I said.

Light of the heart,
The wheat had started lighting its lanterns,
And in every house in heaven there were lights waving
Hello good-bye. But that's
Another life.
Snug on the crumbling earth
The old bottles lay dreaming of new wine.
I picked up my breast, which had gone out.
By other lights I go looking for yours

Through the standing harvest of my lost arrows.
Under the moon the shadow
Practices mowing. Not for me, I say,
Please not for my
Benefit. A man cannot live by bread
Alone.


NOW AND AGAIN


Now that summer is lying with a stone for a lantern
You would think we could keep our thoughts
On the eyes of the living,

Those refugees,

Webs without spiders, needs without choice,
Lakes behind grids but without maps
Into which nothing keeps dropping like a stone.

Even our own.

Even the heart, that closed eye,
Has had its glimpses,
So that the marbled lid winced and fluttered.

You would think we would know the present when it came,
And would remember what we knew,

And would recognize its fish-eyed children, able
To stare through tears forever
Not knowing them for sorrow and their own.

When you consider how learning happens
You would think once might be enough.
You would suppose such pain would become knowledge
And such knowledge would be wisdom
And such wisdom would stay with us.

Each time
The leaves hesitate but finally they fall.

The stars that came with us this far have gone back.
The wings of the migrants wake into autumn, and through
The hammered leaves the walnuts
Drop to the road and open:
Here is the small brain of our extinct summer.
Already it remembers nothing.

## ANOTHER YEAR COME

I have nothing new to ask of you,
Future, heaven of the poor.
I am still wearing the same things.

I am still begging the same question
By the same light,
Eating the same stone,

And the hands of the clock still knock without entering.


## OCTOBER

I remember how I would say, "I will gather
These pieces together,
Any minute now I will make
A knife out of a cloud."
Even then the days
Went leaving their wounds behind them,
But, "Monument," I kept saying to the grave,
"I am still your legend."

There was another time
When our hands met and the clocks struck
And we lived on the point of a needle, like angels.

I have seen the spider's triumph
In the palm of my hand. Above
My grave, that thoroughfare,
There are words now that can bring
My eyes to my feet, tamed.
Beyond the trees wearing names that are not their own
The paths are growing like smoke.

The promises have gone,
Gone, gone, and they were here just now.
There is the sky where they laid their fish.
Soon it will be evening.


## DEPARTURE'S GIRL-FRIEND


Loneliness leapt in the mirrors, but all week
I kept them covered like cages. Then I thought
Of a better thing.

And though it was late night in the city
There I was on my way
To my boat, feeling good to be going, hugging
This big wreath with the words like real
Silver: *Bon Voyage.*

    The night
Was mine but everyone's, like a birthday.
Its fur touched my face in passing. I was going
Down to my boat, my boat,
To see it off, and glad at the thought.
Some leaves of the wreath were holding my hands
And the rest waved good-bye as I walked, as though
They were still alive.

And all went well till I came to the wharf, and no one.

I say no one, but I mean
There was this young man, maybe
Out of the merchant marine,
In some uniform, and I knew who he was; just the same
When he said to me where do you think you're going,
I was happy to tell him.

But he said to me, it isn't your boat,
You don't have one. I said, it's mine, I can prove it:
Look at this wreath I'm carrying to it,
*Bon Voyage.* He said, this is the stone wharf, lady,
You don't own anything here.
                                        And as I
Was turning away, the injustice of it
Lit up the buildings, and there I was
In the other and hated city
Where I was born, where nothing is moored, where
The lights crawl over the stone like flies, spelling now,
Now, and the same fat chances roll
Their many eyes; and I step once more
Through a hoop of tears and walk on, holding this
Buoy of flowers in front of my beauty,
Wishing myself the good voyage.


ONE WAY


Oh hell, there once again hunger
Gets up in the middle of a meal and without
A word departs. I go after: what
Would I be without her?

                                        It is
Night, I am
As old as pain and I have
No other story.
We do not keep to the telegraph lines.
"Is there a map for this?" I call
After. "Is there even
A name for this? I spend my
Life asking, is there even a name
For you?"

And what a starved path,
Licking stones; often
I am sure one side has eaten the other.
And with what bitterness I remember
I had not yet had my fill
Of dissatisfaction. My mouth
Works like a heart. More and more
I get like shadows; I find out
How they hate.
                    And then she is gone.


No astonishment anywhere. The owls
Are digesting in silence.
I will not look up again to learn again
That despair has no star.
Don't ask me why, I
Lift my feet in their dice-boxes.
I believe I continue
As she would have done, I believe.


                              Don't ask me
Why: this time it is not I
Waking the birds. Somewhere
The light begins to come to itself.
As I walk, the horizon
Climbs down from its tree and moves toward me
With offerings. There
At the table which she has set with
The old plates, she is waiting, and to us
The day returns like a friend
Bringing others.

# RECOGNITION

The bird of ash has appeared at windows
And the roads will turn away, mourning.
What distances we survived, the fire
With its one wing
And I with my blackened heart.

I came home as a web to its spider,
To teach the flies of my household
Their songs. I walked
In on the mirrors scarred as match-boxes,
The gaze of the frames and the ticking
In the beams. The shadows
Had grown a lot and they clung
To the skirts of the lamps.
Nothing
Remembered who I was.

The dead turn in their locks and
I wake like a hand on a handle. Tomorrow
Marches on the old walls, and there
Is my coat full of darkness in its place
On the door.
Welcome home,
Memory.

## INVOCATION

The day hanging by its feet with a hole
In its voice
And the light running into the sand

Here I am once again with my dry mouth
At the fountain of thistles
Preparing to sing.


## THE POEM

Coming late, as always,
I try to remember what I almost heard.
The light avoids my eye.

How many times have I heard the locks close
And the lark take the keys
And hang them in heaven.


## SECOND SIGHT

Turning the corner I
Realize that I have read this before.
It is summer. The sun
Sits on the fire-escape while its children
Tear their voices into little shreds.
I wish I could remember how it ended.

This is the passage where the mirrors
Are embarking at the ends of the streets.

The drawn shades are waving
From empty rooms, and the old days
Are fanning themselves here and there on the steps.
The fact is, I have come back
Again and again, as a wish on a postcard, only
This time the jewels are turning
In the faces, and it seems I should know
The motive for the laundry, and the name
Of the man with the teeth, at intervals saying
You want to buy your time.

I feel this is a bit that I know how it goes;
I should be able to call
Most of the windows
By their Christian names, they have whole
Chapters to themselves
Before the pigeons give up, and the brightest
Are reflections of darkness. But no,
They've got it wrong, they've got it wrong,
Like anywhere else.

It's the old story,
Every morning something different is real.
This place is no more than the nephew of itself,
With these cats, this traffic, these
Departures
To which I have kept returning,
Having tasted the apple of my eye,
Saying perennially
Here it is, the one and only,
The beginning and the end.
This time the dials have come with the hands and
Suddenly I was never here before.
Oh dust, oh dust, progress
Is being made.

## WITNESSES

Evening has brought its
Mouse and let it out on the floor,
On the wall, on the curtain, on
The clock. You with the gloves, in the doorway,
Who asked you to come and watch?

As the bats flower in the crevices
You and your brothers
Raise your knives to see by.
Surely the moon can find her way to the wells
Without you. And the streams
To their altars.

As for us, we enter your country
With our eyes closed.

## THE INDIGESTION OF THE VAMPIRE

Look at this red pear
Hanging from a good family

Where the butcher hung the rag on the tree.

The bat's bloated again,
Hooked on his dark nimbus
Getting over it.
Here is the cure of pity
Upside down.

Elsewhere the laundry
Is buried,
The deer tracks left by his teeth

Look for the crossroads,
The veins that are still good
Hold out their hands.

                   Here's his story.

His bridges are not burned only folded.
In a while the swollen life
He calls his own
Will shrink back till it fits the mirrors,
No worse for no wear;
The eyes will come
To conceal movement again;
He will find his voice to fly by.

That's how he does it: rock-a-bye,
Hanging there with his silence all wool
And others at heart,
Two pounds in his pound bag,

Shaped like a tear but
Not falling for anyone.

## THE SINGER

The song dripping from the eaves,
I know that throat

With no tongue,
Ignoring sun and moon,

That glance, that creature
Returning to its heart

By whose light the streams
Find each other.

Untameable,
Incorruptible,

In its own country
It has a gate to guard.

There arrived without choice
Take up water

And lay it on your eyes saying
Hail clarity

From now on nothing
Will appear the same

And pass through
Leaving your salt behind.


## THE CONTINUO


What can you do with this
Wind, you can't
Reason with it, entertain it, send
It back, live on it or with it, fold it
Away and forget it, coming at you

All the time perfectly
Empty no face no background,
Before you know it, needing
No doors,
Lighting out of trees, flags, windows of
Fallen buildings, with a noise that could
Run its own trains, what
Can you learn from it

Leaving its shoes all over the place
Turning day and night into
Back yards
Where it knows the way.


VOCATIONS


I

Simplicity, if you
Have any time
Where do you spend it?
I tempt you with clear water.
All day I hang out a blue eye. All night
I long for the sound of your small bell
Of an unknown metal.


II

Seeing how it goes
I see how it will be:
The color leaves but the light stays,
The light stays but we cannot grasp it.
We leave the tree rocking its
Head in its hands and we
Go indoors.


III

The locked doors of the night were still sitting in their circle.
I recalled the promises of the bridges.
I got up and made my way
To wash my shadow in the river.
In a direction that was lost
The hands of the water have found tomorrow.

# AIR

Naturally it is night.
Under the overturned lute with its
One string I am going my way
Which has a strange sound.

This way the dust, that way the dust.
I listen to both sides
But I keep right on.
I remember the leaves sitting in judgment
And then winter.

I remember the rain with its bundle of roads.
The rain taking all its roads.
Nowhere.

Young as I am, old as I am,

I forget tomorrow, the blind man.
I forget the life among the buried windows.
The eyes in the curtains.
The wall
Growing through the immortelles.
I forget silence
The owner of the smile.

This must be what I wanted to be doing,
Walking at night between the two deserts,
Singing.

## THE PRESENT

The walls join hands and
It is tomorrow:
The birds clucking to the horses, the horses
Doing the numbers for the hell of it,
The numbers playing the calendars,
The saints marching in,
It seems only yesterday,
                    when what
I keep saying to myself is
Take a leaf from the fire, open
Your hand, see
Where you are going,
When what I am trying to find is
The beginning,
In the ashes,
A wing, when what we are looking for
In each other
Is each other,

The stars at noon,

While the light worships its blind god.


## STANDARDS

Nothing will do but
I must get a new flag,
I've buried enough under this one,

And then there are my
Followers, mad for a bit of color,
Damn them,

And the end I suppose is not yet,
The way the trees come beating
Their horses, and the wheat is camped
Under its dead crow,
The rivers under themselves. And I'm not ready
To just sit down and let the horizon
Ride over me.

Maybe I thought
I could go on and on flying the same rag,
Like the fire,
But it's faded white and I'm
Not the fire, I'll have to find
Something bright and simple to signify
Me, what an order.

What an order but I'll have to do something.
Up until now the pulse
Of a stone was my flag
And the stone's in pieces.


FROM A SERIES


Division, mother of pain,
Look at you bringing
Your children up just as formerly
And look at me back again
In this former life,
You've all grown but I haven't.

You might as well ask me why
I come back to a month
All right
Why do I and when I think

There used to be eleven others
At one time as they say and those
Other days in the week
I see the posters have changed
But the day's the same and even
When it was here hope would wait
Out in the garden rocking the grave
Now she's dead too and that's a blessing.

Just the same it was nice the way
You had them trained
And as for me it was nice
The way I used to be able
To forget between
The last time I learned and the next time;
The way I loved
The east and the west my horses;
It had its points, surely, if only
I could have been one at a time.
How long

Can the hands of the clock go on drowning
Without my helping
One way or the other
How long
Before freedom looms in front of me
And the door falls in on my tongue?


BREAD AND BUTTER


I keep finding this letter
To the gods of abandon,
Tearing it up: Sirs,
Having lived in your shrines
I know what I owe you —

I don't, did I ever? With both hands
I've forgotten, I keep
Having forgotten. I'll have no such shrines here.
I will not bow in the middle of the room
To the statue of nothing
With the flies turning around it.
On these four walls I am the writing.

Why would I start such a letter?
Think of today, think of tomorrow.
Today on the tip of my tongue,
Today with my eyes,
Tomorrow the vision,
Tomorrow

In the broken window
The broken boats will come in,
The life boats
Waving their severed hands,

And I will love as I ought to
Since the beginning.

WE CONTINUE

*for Galway Kinnell*

The rust, a little pile of western color, lies
At the end of its travels,
Our instrument no longer.

Those who believe
In death have their worship cut out for them.
As for myself, we
Continue,

An old
Scar of light our trumpet,

Pilgrims with thorns
To the eye of the cold
Under flags made by the blind,
In one fist

This letter that vanishes
If the hand opens:

*Charity, come home,*
*Begin.*


MARICA LART


Now
We do not even know
What to wish for you

Oh sleep rocked
In an empty hand.


REUNION


At the foot of your dry well,
Old friend in ambush,
What did we expect?

Have we really changed?
You could never forgive me for
Pleasures divulged or defeats kept secret.

You have flowered in your little heat
Like an untrimmed wick.
It is plain what you are thinking

While I am thinking
How you have grown into your ugliness
Which at one time did not fit you.

Console your distaste for departures:
I find I brought only the one.
Hand me my coat.

Friend Reductio,
Would you have known delight
If it had knocked you down?


WALK-UP


The inspector of stairs is on the stairs
Oh my God and I thought it was Sunday,
His advance like a broom and those stairs going
Down to meet him, all right
What that's mine will he show me
To be ashamed of this time

The spiders in my face, the whistles
In the cupboards,
The darkness in my shoes, going out
To deep water

No

The sky's at home in these windows, and the maps
Of themselves on these walls,

And your letter is enough improvement
For anywhere, lying open
On my table, my
Love

    I won't close a thing

Let him arrive fanning himself
With his calendar, let him become
At the door the inspector of doors and find
Mine open,
Inspector of hands –

        His name
Would mean nothing to me, his questions are not
His own, but let my answers
Be mine.


## TO WHERE WE ARE


With open arms the water runs in to the wheel.

I come back to where I have never been.
You arrive to join me.
We have the date in our hands.

We come on to where we are, laughing to think
Of the Simplicities in their shapeless hats
With a door so they can sit outside it

I hope I may say
Our neighbors

Natives of now, creatures of
One song,
Their first, their last,

Listen.


## THE CROSSROADS OF THE WORLD ETC.


I would never have thought I would be born here

So late in the stone so long before morning
Between the rivers learning of salt

Memory my city

Hope my city Ignorance my city
With my teeth on your chessboard black and white
What is your name

With my dead on your
Calendar with my eyes
In your paint
Opening
With my grief on your bridges with my voice
In your stones what is your name
Typed in rain while I slept

The books just give
The names of locks
The old books names of old locks
Some have stopped beating

Photos of
Dead doors left to right still hide
The beginning

Which do you
Open if
Any
My shadow crosses them trying to strike a light

Today is in another street

I'm coming to that
Before me

The bird of the end with its
Colorless feet
Has walked on windows

I lose the track but I find it
Again again
Memory

In the mirrors the star called Nothing

Cuts us off

Wait for me

Ruin
My city
Oh wreck of the future out of which
The future rises
What is your name as we fall

As the mortar
Falls between the faces
As the one-legged man watching the chess game

Falls
As the moon withers in the blueprint
And from our graves these curtains blow

These clouds on which I have written
Hope

As I
Have done
Hearing the light flowing over a knife
And autumn on the posters

Hearing a shadow beating a bell
Ice cream in ambulances, a chain full of fingers
The trains on the
Trestles faster than their lights
The new scars around the bend
Arriving

Hearing the day pass talking to itself
Again
Another life

Once a key in another country
Now ignorance
Ignorance

I keep to your streets until they vanish
There is singing beyond
The addresses can I
Let it go home alone

A playing on veins a lark in a lantern

It conducts me to a raw Sabbath

On all sides bread
Has been begged, here are monuments
At their feet this
Section
The tubes tied off the cry gone

The cry
I would never have thought
The lightning rises and sets

Rust, my brothers, stone, my brothers
Hung your spirits on the high hooks
Can't reach them now

You've swallowed night I swallow night
I will swallow night
And lie among the games of papers
And the gills of nibbling
Fires

Will I

While the sky waits in the station like a man
With no place to go

Will I

I hear my feet in a tunnel but I move
Like a tear on a doorsill
It's now in my wrist

Ahead of me under
False teeth hanging from a cloud, his
Sign that digs for his house, Tomorrow,
The oldest man
Is throwing food into empty cages

Is it to me
He turns his cobweb
I go toward him extending
My shadow taking it to him
Is it to me he says no

Is it to me
He says no no I haven't time

Keep the lost garment, where would I find the owner?


## RESOLUTION

Back of the door the child is playing that
Piano drawn on a piece of paper
He keeps to the black notes it
Gets dark
He moves to the white notes it gets
Too dark I can't hear him any more

As I was

The customs men multiply between
He takes with him
Memory leaking feathers
If he knew what I
Know now in the same X-ray

The pictures turn to the walls here is
Death the same taste in
A different color
Thinks I will say it

The scars
Grow leaves the feeling
Runs ahead and hides in bushes with its
Knives painted out
I know

Thinks I will say
It say it
As the hole climbs the sky

*Oh let it be yesterday surely*
*It's time*

Never

Never

A usage I'm learning a beak at my ear
I hear

The hearts in bottles
The dice lying awake

The clock dropping its shoes and
No floor


BEFORE THAT


It was never there and already it's vanishing

City unhealthy pale with pictures of
    Cemeteries sifting on its windows
    Its planets with wind in their eyes searching among
    The crosses again
    At night
    In dark clothes

    It was never there

    Papers news from the desert
    Moving on or
    Lying in cages
    Wrapping for their
    Voices

The river flowing past its other shore
Past the No Names the windows washed at night
And who is my
Name for

In my pocket
Slowly the photographs becoming saints
Never there

I put out my hand and the dark falls through it
Following a flag

Gutters made in my time rounded with
The wounded in mind
The streets roped off for the affectionate
Will do for the
Mutilated

If I
Lie down in the street and that smoke comes out of me

Who
Was it

It was a night like this that the ashes were made

Before that
Was always the fire

## FOR THE GRAVE OF POSTERITY

This stone that is
not here and bears no writing commemorates
the emptiness at the end of
history listen you without vision you can still

hear it there is
nothing it is the voice with the praises
that never changed that called to the unsatisfied
as long as there was
time
whatever it could have said of you is already forgotten


THIS DAY OF THIS MONTH OF THIS YEAR OF THIS


How can I persuade today that it's
                    Here how can I
Say    My
       Love

       Outlined in knives

       I'm tracing you with an
       Opened finger the eye
       Of my thumb is away
                    Is not
       This your home where are you
       Is not this
       Your home

       Drunks on the compass feathers on the floor yes here

       Where the river flows around our suitcases
       Where the light shakes the buildings
       Where they teach silence in both schools on this block but
       The streets give
                    Cry give cry all the time

       Where Easter the phantom hounds the Holy Rollers
       Where the months are shot at midnight by
       A cop in civvies in a dark car on a side street

Where my birth came upon me comes upon me where

My hand that found the hand
Of day finds the hand of
Absence

Where my arm is smoke

Before the two cripples pass on their one crutch
Before the spittle rises from the sidewalk
Before the darkness comes out of the
Trumpet
Tunnel to itself subway with
No platform

                              I want
To declare myself

I want to declare Now

Her name is now wherever she is
            There is none beside her

            For whom my hands were split
I want
To make time with her under the same flag
Running water with running water I want
To point out the sights ahead of us would
There be sights ahead of us

With my story

With the child I left to die
                  Dying
With the love I wrapped in a map
                  There

With the uniform I wore
                    Black
                    As they all are

With my teeth graveyard for the nameless
With extinction my ancestor
With a fresh sparrow caught in the headlines
With the funerals in the bridges
                    From which the music
                    With
My lungs full of ashes
With what I empty from my shoes

With the other calendar other
            Facade in which I have a darkness
            Marked X to which my key marked X

            X in my hand in both hands
            X waiting

Oh with
            Death testing itself in my ocean cream in my coffee
            Death my window at which the birds come to drink at night

Oh with your face her face your
Face invisible

With death my hands

With my hands nothing oh with death my words

With my words nothing
One at a time

Oh with death my
Heart
With my heart

Lantern of ice

Oh with her shoes
        Hanging
        In the clock


## THE WAY TO THE RIVER


The way to the river leads past the names of
Ash the sleeves the wreaths of hinges
Through the song of the bandage vendor

I lay your name by my voice
As I go

The way to the river leads past the late
Doors and the games of the children born looking backwards
They play that they are broken glass
The numbers wait in the halls and the clouds
Call
From windows
They play that they are old they are putting the horizon
Into baskets they are escaping they are
Hiding

I step over the sleepers the fires the calendars
My voice turns to you

I go past the juggler's condemned building the hollow
Windows gallery
Of invisible presidents the same motion in them all
In a parked cab by the sealed wall the hats are playing
Sort of poker with somebody's

Old snapshots game I don't understand they lose
The rivers one
After the other I begin to know where I am
I am home

Be here the flies from the house of the mapmaker
Walk on our letters I can tell
And the days hang medals between us
I have lit our room with a glove of yours be
Here I turn
To your name and the hour remembers
Its one word
Now

Be here what can we
Do for the dead the footsteps full of money
I offer you what I have my
Poverty

To the city of wires I have brought home a handful
Of water I walk slowly
In front of me they are building the empty
Ages I see them reflected not for long
Be here I am no longer ashamed of time it is too brief its hands
Have no names
I have passed it I know

> *Oh Necessity you with the face you with*
> *All the faces*

This is written on the back of everything

But we
Will read it together

## SHE WHO WAS GONE

Passage of lights without hands
Passage of hands without lights
This water between

I take in my arms

My love whose names I cannot say
Not knowing them and having a tongue
Of dust

My love with light flowing on her like tears

She on whom the bruise went sailing
She who was a shoe on a pillow
She who was gone

Under empty socks hanging mouth downward from the bridges
Under the color of no one
While feathers went on falling in the doorways

She who with a blank ticket waited
Under a flag made of flies while the sun brought
Blood in eyecups

I take in my arms

My love from the valley of dice my love in the valley of dice
Among the flowers smelling of lightning
My love on whom the light has forgotten nothing

We say good-bye distance we are here
We can say it quietly who else is there
We can say it with silence our native tongue

MY FRIENDS

My friends without shields walk on the target

It is late the windows are breaking

My friends without shoes leave
What they love
Grief moves among them as a fire among
Its bells
My friends without clocks turn
On the dial they turn
They part

My friends with names like gloves set out
Bare handed as they have lived
And nobody knows them
It is they that lay the wreaths at the milestones it is their
Cups that are found at the wells
And are then chained up

My friends without feet sit by the wall
Nodding to the lame orchestra
*Brotherhood* it says on the decorations
My friend without eyes sits in the rain smiling
With a nest of salt in his hand

My friends without fathers or houses hear
Doors opening in the darkness
Whose halls announce
Behold the smoke has come home

My friends and I have in common
The present a wax bell in a wax belfry
This message telling of
Metals this
Hunger for the sake of hunger this owl in the heart

And these hands one
For asking one for applause

My friends with nothing leave it behind
In a box
My friends without keys go out from the jails it is night
They take the same road they miss
Each other they invent the same banner in the dark
They ask their way only of sentries too proud to breathe

At dawn the stars on their flag will vanish

The water will turn up their footprints and the day will rise
Like a monument to my
Friends the forgotten


THE MAN WHO WRITES ANTS


Their eggs named for his eyes I suppose
Their eggs his tears
His memory
                Into
The ground into the walls over the sills

At each cross road
He has gone

With his days he has gone ahead
        Called by what trumpet

His words on the signs
His tears at their feet
        Growing wings

I know him from tunnels by side roads
I know him

Not his face if he has one

I know him by his writings I am
Tempted to draw him
As I see him
Sandals stride flag on his shoulder ship on it signaling
Mask on the back of his head
Blind

Called

By what trumpet

He leaves my eyes he climbs my graves
I pass the names

He is not followed I am not following him no

Today the day of the water
With ink for my remote purpose with my pockets full of black
With no one in sight
I am walking in silence I am walking in silence I am walking
In single file listening for a trumpet


THE NEXT


The funeral procession swinging empty belts
Walks on the road on the black rain
Though the one who is dead was not ready

In the casket lid the nails are still turning

Behind it come the bearers
Of tires and wet pillows and the charred ladder
And the unrollers of torn music and a picture of smoke
And last the boy trailing the long
String cut off clean
Whom a voice follows calling Why a white one
When a red one would have done just as well

Under the casket the number
Is scratched out with signs of haste

We let it go we gather with other persuaders
In the parlor of the house of The Next
And I in my wax shoes my mind goes back
To the last dead Who was it I say

Could it have been my friend the old man
With the wet dog and the shed where he
Slept on a ladder till the whole place burned
Here just now was his other
Friend the carpenter
Who was besides a crusher of shells for cement
No they say he was months ago this was no one we knew
But he was one of us

We let it go we are
Gathered with other persuaders in the parlor
The Next is upstairs he is
Ten feet tall hale and solid his bed is no deathbed
He is surrounded by friends they enjoy the secret of safety
They are flush they are candle-lit they move to laughter
Downstairs it is not yet known
Who will go instead of him this time
Like the others one after the other because they were scared

The laughter keeps time on the stairs

These words start rising out of my wax shoes I
Say we must tell him
We must go up there we must go up there and You
Are The Next we must tell him
The persuaders say he would deafen us
When we say No no one hears us

My shoes are softening but at the same time I am saying
Someone would help us and it would be us
Even the carpenter would
Help us when he went out he said
He would not be gone long
Removing a knocker from a door
And the caskets are clearly numbered not ours we
Must rise under the turning nails
I say to the persuaders downstairs in the house of The Next

And when they say Yes no one hears them


## THE STUDENTS OF JUSTICE


All night I hear the hammers
Of the blind men in the next building
Repairing their broken doors

When it is silent it is
That they are gone
Before the sun lights the way for
The young thieves

All day the blind neighbors are at their lesson
Coloring a rough book
Oh a long story
And under their white hair they keep forgetting

It tells of gorges hung with high caves and
Little rotting flags
And through the passes caravans of bugs
Bearing away our blood in pieces

What can be done what can be done

They take their hammers to the lesson

The last words so they promise me
Will be thank you and they will know why

And that night they will be allowed to move

Every day
They leave me their keys which they never use


AN ISLAND IN THE HARBOR


My own country my countrymen the exchanges
Yes this is the place

The flag of the blank wall the birds of money

Prisoners in the watch towers
And the motto
>           *The hopes of others our*
>           *Guardians*

Even here
Spring passes looking for the cradles

The beating on the bars of the cages
Is caught and parceled out to the bells

It is twelve the prisoners' own hour

The mouse bones in the plaster
Prepare for the resurrection


MOUNTAIN TOWN


My memory the invisible buffalo
Lumbers through the vacant street
Considering the fences their

Sorrows

And the lightning died in its
Mine oh it must be
Some time back its name
Is written everywhere in faded
Dust

One of its
Gloves wheels on the sky over
The blind movie
And the station where the white train still
Attends

A bell that I hung onto as long as I could
Is about to arrive and start ringing

## FOR NOW

The year a bird flies against the drum

I come to myself miles away with
Tickets dying in my hand

You are not here will the earth last till you come
I must say now what cannot
Be said later Goodbye
The name of the statues but who needs them
As for myself I

Look back at the rain
I grew up in the rooms of the rain
So that was home so let the grass grow
Goodbye faces in stains churches
In echoes dusters at windows
Schools without floors envelopes full of smoke
Goodbye hands of those days I keep the fossils
Goodbye iron Bible containing my name in rust
Cock Robin and
The date
Goodbye Cock Robin I never saw you

On plates upside down in token of mourning
I eat to your vanishing

I bearing messages
With all my words my silence being one

From childhood to childhood the
Message Goodbye from the shoulders of victory
To the followers
From the sea to the nearest of kin

From the roller skates to the death in the basement
From the lightning to
Its nest from myself to my name
Goodbye

I begin with what was always gone

Ancestors in graves of broken glass
In empty cameras

Mistakes in the mail Goodbye to the same name

Goodbye what you learned for me I have to learn anyway

You that forgot your rivers they are gone
Myself I would not know you

Goodbye as
The eyes of a whale say goodbye having never seen
Each other

And to you that vanished as I watched goodbye
Walter the First
Jacques the Clown
Marica the Good

Goodbye pain of the past that
Will never be made better goodbye
Pain of the innocent that will never
Not have existed
Goodbye you that are
Buried with the name of the florist in your hands
And a box from our
Box society your finger holding the place
Your jaws tied with a ribbon marked Justice
To help us

The dead say Look
The living in their distress sink upward weeping
But who could reach them in such a sea

Goodbye kites painted with open mouths over the
Scarlet road of the animals

Goodbye prophets sometimes we are
Here sometimes we remember it
Sometimes we walk in your
Eyes which sometimes you lost
Sometimes we walk in your old brains and are forgotten

Or this character gets on the bus with an open razor
Bends down to my face at once thinking he
Knows me goodbye
Yard where I was supposed
To be safe behind the fences of sand
Watched over by an empty parasol and the sound of
Pulleys I who
Had built the ark

Goodbye cement street address of cement tears
Grief of the wallpaper the witness
Cold banisters worn thin with fright
Photo of me wondering what it would be like
The girls at last the hips full of dice the names
In smoke for the lamps the
Calling Goodbye among the wishes
Among the horses

If I had known what to say there would be the same hands
Holding white crosses in front of the windows

Goodbye to the dew my master

And you masters with feathers on your key rings
Wardens of empty scales
When I find where I am goodbye

Goodbye sound of a voice spelling its name to a uniform
Spelling it
Again goodbye white
Truck that backs up to drugstores after dark
Arriving at
Apartment houses in the afternoon
And the neighbors calling can you come up for a minute

Goodbye anniversaries I pass without knowing
Days for which the chairs are wired
The law on the throne of ice above the salting floor
Its eyes full of falling snow
Friend Instead and the rest of the
Brothers Meaningless
Those who will drown next bow to their straws

Goodbye to the water a happy person
The longer its story the
Less it tells
Goodbye to the numbers starting with God

To the avenues
No one asked their permission so they had none

Goodbye hands wrapped in newspaper

And when the towers are finished the frameworks are
Thrown from the tops and descend slowly
Waving as they
Dissolve

Tell me what you see vanishing and I
Will tell you who you are
To whom I say Goodbye

You my neighbors in the windows in the registers you
The sizes of your clothes
You born with the faces of presidents on your eyelids

Tell me how your hands fall and I will tell you
What you will wave to next
Guests of yourselves expecting hosts
You in the cold of whose
Voices I can hear
The hanged man in the chimney turning
You with mouths full of pebbles
In the rising elevator in the falling building you
With your destinations written in your shoelaces
And your lies elected

They return in the same
Skins to the same seats by the flags of money
Goodbye to the Bibles hollowed for swearing on
A hole knocks on the panes but is not heard

Around them the crashes occur in silence
The darkness that flows from the sirens passes the windows
The blackness spreads from the headlines
Over their spectacles they light the ceilings

Goodbye what we may never see
Age would have kissed false teeth if any
Its caresses making a bed slowly
Even as a child I hoped it would spare me
I made tears for it I sang

As the cards are laid out they turn to ashes
I kiss
The light to those who love it it is brief

Goodbye before it is taken away
I have been with it the season could sign for me

The message sang in its bottle it would find me
I knew the king of the moths I knew the watchman's country
I knew where the phoebe lost herself I knew the story
I stepped in the lock I
Turned
My thumb was carved with the one map of a lost mountain
My scars will answer to no one but me
I know the planet that lights up the rings in the hems
I know the stars in the door

I know the martyrs sleeping in almonds
I know the gloves of the hours I know Pilate the fly
I know the enemy's brother

But it will happen just the same goodbye

Heart my elder

My habits of sand
My bones whose count is lost every night every day
The milestones of salt the rain my feet
Memory in its rivers
Goodbye my house my cat my spiders

Goodbye distance from whom I
Borrow my eyes goodbye my voice
In the monument of strangers goodbye to the sun
Among the wings nailed to the window goodbye
My love

You that return to me through the mountain of flags
With my raven on your wrist
You with the same breath

Between death's republic and his kingdom

SPRING

On the water the first wind
Breaks it all up into arrows

The dead bowmen buried these many years

Are setting out again

And I
I take down from the door
My story with the holes
For the arms the face and the vitals
I take down the sights from the mantle
I'm going to my uncle the honest one
Who stole me the horse in the good cause

There's light in my shoes
I carry my bones on a drum
I'm going to my uncle the dog
The croupier the old horror
The one who takes me as I am

Like the rest of the devils he was born in heaven

Oh withered rain

Tears of the candles veins full of feathers
Knees in salt
I the bell's only son

Having spent one day in his house
Will have your answer

## DAYBREAK

Again this procession of the speechless
Bringing me their words
The future woke me with its silence
I join the procession
An open doorway
Speaks for me
Again

# THE

# LICE

## (1967)

*All men are deceived by the appearances of things, even Homer himself, who was the wisest man in Greece; for he was deceived by boys catching lice: they said to him, "What we have caught and what we have killed we have left behind, but what has escaped us we bring with us."*

HERACLITUS

## THE ANIMALS

All these years behind windows
With blind crosses sweeping the tables

And myself tracking over empty ground
Animals I never saw

I with no voice

Remembering names to invent for them
Will any come back will one

Saying yes

Saying look carefully yes
We will meet again


## IS THAT WHAT YOU ARE

New ghost is that what you are
Standing on the stairs of water

No longer surprised

Hope and grief are still our wings
Why we cannot fly

What failure still keeps you
Among us the unfinished

The wheels go on praying

We are not hearing something different
We beat our wings
Why are you there

I did not think I had anything else to give

The wheels say it after me

There are feathers in the ice
We lay the cold across our knees

Today the sun is farther than we think

And at the windows in the knives
You are watching


THE HYDRA


No no the dead have no brothers

The Hydra calls me but I am used to it
It calls me Everybody
But I know my name and do not answer

And you the dead
You know your names as I do not
But at moments you have just finished speaking

The snow stirs in its wrappings
Every season comes from a new place

Like your voice with its resemblances

A long time ago the lightning was practising
Something I thought was easy

I was young and the dead were in other
Ages
As the grass had its own language

Now I forget where the difference falls

One thing about the living sometimes a piece of us
Can stop dying for a moment
But you the dead

Once you go into those names you go on you never
Hesitate
You go on


SOME LAST QUESTIONS


What is the head
                    A. Ash
What are the eyes
                    A. The wells have fallen in and have
                        Inhabitants
What are the feet
                    A. Thumbs left after the auction
No what are the feet
                    A. Under them the impossible road is moving
                        Down which the broken necked mice push
                        Balls of blood with their noses
What is the tongue
                    A. The black coat that fell off the wall
                        With sleeves trying to say something
What are the hands
                    A. Paid

No what are the hands
           A. Climbing back down the museum wall
              To their ancestors the extinct shrews that will
              Have left a message
What is the silence
           A. As though it had a right to more
Who are the compatriots
           A. They make the stars of bone


AN END IN SPRING


It is carried beyond itself a little way
And covered with a sky of old bedding

The compatriots stupid as their tables
Go on eating their packages
Selling gloves to the clocks
Doing all right

Ceasing to exist it becomes a deity

It is with the others that are not there
The centuries are named for them the names
Do not come down to us

On the way to them the words
Die

## I LIVE UP HERE

I live up here
And a little bit to the left
And I go down only

For the accidents and then
Never a moment too soon

Just the same it's a life it's plenty

The stairs the petals she loves me
Every time
Nothing has changed

Oh down there down there
Every time
The glass knights lie by their gloves of blood

In the pans of the scales the helmets
Brim over with water
It's perfectly fair

The pavements are dealt out the dice
Every moment arrive somewhere

You can hear the hearses getting lost in lungs
Their bells stalling
And then silence comes with the plate and I
Give what I can

Feeling *It's worth it*

For I see
What my votes the mice are accomplishing
And I know I'm free

This is how I live
Up here and simply

Others do otherwise
Maybe


## THE LAST ONE


Well they'd made up their minds to be everywhere because why not.
Everywhere was theirs because they thought so.
They with two leaves they whom the birds despise.
In the middle of stones they made up their minds.
They started to cut.

Well they cut everything because why not.
Everything was theirs because they thought so.
It fell into its shadows and they took both away.
Some to have some for burning.

Well cutting everything they came to the water.
They came to the end of the day there was one left standing.
They would cut it tomorrow they went away.
The night gathered in the last branches.
The shadow of the night gathered in the shadow on the water.
The night and the shadow put on the same head.
And it said Now.

Well in the morning they cut the last one.
Like the others the last one fell into its shadow.
It fell into its shadow on the water.
They took it away its shadow stayed on the water.

Well they shrugged they started trying to get the shadow away.
They cut right to the ground the shadow stayed whole.
They laid boards on it the shadow came out on top.

They shone lights on it the shadow got blacker and clearer.
They exploded the water the shadow rocked.
They built a huge fire on the roots.
They sent up black smoke between the shadow and the sun.
The new shadow flowed without changing the old one.
They shrugged they went away to get stones.

They came back the shadow was growing.
They started setting up stones it was growing.
They looked the other way it went on growing.
They decided they would make a stone out of it.
They took stones to the water they poured them into the shadow.
They poured them in they poured them in the stones vanished.
The shadow was not filled it went on growing.
That was one day.

The next day was just the same it went on growing.
They did all the same things it was just the same.
They decided to take its water from under it.
They took away water they took it away the water went down.
The shadow stayed where it was before.
It went on growing it grew onto the land.
They started to scrape the shadow with machines.
When it touched the machines it stayed on them.
They started to beat the shadow with sticks.
Where it touched the sticks it stayed on them.
They started to beat the shadow with hands.
Where it touched the hands it stayed on them.
That was another day.

Well the next day started about the same it went on growing.
They pushed lights into the shadow.
Where the shadow got onto them they went out.
They began to stomp on the edge it got their feet.
And when it got their feet they fell down.
It got into eyes the eyes went blind.

The ones that fell down it grew over and they vanished.

The ones that went blind and walked into it vanished.
The ones that could see and stood still
It swallowed their shadows.
Then it swallowed them too and they vanished.
Well the others ran.

The ones that were left went away to live if it would let them.
They went as far as they could.
The lucky ones with their shadows.


# UNFINISHED BOOK OF KINGS

### ALPHA

I  In all the teeth Death turned over

II  And the new whistles called for the first time in the streets before daybreak

III  Silence the last of the liberty ships had come up the river during the night and tied up to wait until the wharf rotted away

IV  At that time the civil war between the dynasties of absence had been going on for many years

V  But during that winter the lips of the last prophets had fallen from the last trees

VI  They had fallen without a sound they had not stayed in spite of the assurances proceeding from the mouths of the presidents in the money pinned thick as tobacco fish over the eyes of the saints

VII  And in spite of the little votes burning at the altars in front of the empty walls

VIII  And the jailers' eagle headed keys renewed in the name of freedom

IX  It had been many years since the final prophet had felt the hand of the future how it had no weight and had realized that he the prophet was

a ghost and had climbed the cracks in the light to take his place with
the others

   x  The fingers of the prophets fell but were not visible because they
wore no rings

   xi  The feet of the prophets fell but were not visible since their goal had
ceased to exist

   xii  The hearts of the prophets fell out of the old nests

   xiii  The eyes of the prophets fell and broke like rain and a people blind as
hammers hurried through them in their thin shoes

   xiv  The ears of the prophets fell and after that there had been no one to
hear Death saying But I keep trying to remember when I was young


BETA

   i  Before daybreak in the museums the skeletons of extinct horses held
up the skeletons of extinct leaves to listen

   ii  The light was that of the insides of quills and through it the legends
of Accident the hero were marching away down roads that had not
been there since the last free election

   iii  Out of the morning stars the blood began to run down the white sky
and the crowd in tears remembered who they were and raised their
hands shouting Tomorrow our flag

   iv  The lips of the extinct prophets still lay on the ground here and there
murmuring So much for the hair of the moon

   v  But all that really remained of the prophets was their hunger which
continued to fall among the people like invisible fish lines without
hooks

   vi  And morning the carpet bagger arrived with news of victories

   vii  The lovers of flutes embraced the lovers of drums again as though
they trusted them

   viii  The balloon went up that said The day is ours

   I  It had been discovered that the bread was photographs of unidentified seas and not for everyone but it was all taken care of it was put in the banks with the dead

   II  It had been discovered that the bitterness of certain rivers had no source but was caused by their looking for something through the darkness and finding

  III  Something lower

  IV  But it was taken care of the discovery was allowed to die of its own accord

   V  And Distance with his gaunt singers sat among the citizens unnoticed and never distinctly heard

  VI  He stood under the posters advertising the endless newsreels of the deposition and nobody recognized him

 VII  He went into the museums and sat in the undusted replicas of what was said to have been his crown and nobody saw him

VIII  He conducted a chorus of forgiveness for his poor relations the rulers

  IX  Whose blessing was as the folding and unfolding of papers


DELTA

   I  Came the heralds with brushes

  II  Came the rats dragging their leashes some time before the soldiers

  III  Came the cripples walking on separate seas bearing on a long scroll the bill of suffering the signatures the crosses

  IV  Came the bearers of doors of wood and of glass came the eyes with dead wicks came the mourners with their inventories

   V  Cheers cheers but it was only a rehearsal

  VI  Yet the spirit was there and in full daylight voices of dogs were lit on

the hills nibbled coins were flung from balconies and the matches
tipped with blood were brought out and kept handy

VII  The pictures of dead forbears were propped up at windows to be
proud

VIII  The darkness began to dance in the gloves and the cry caught on We
have waited enough war or no war

IX  Calling for the coronation of Their Own the last of the absences


IT IS MARCH


It is March and black dust falls out of the books
Soon I will be gone
The tall spirit who lodged here has
Left already
On the avenues the colorless thread lies under
Old prices

When you look back there is always the past
Even when it has vanished
But when you look forward
With your dirty knuckles and the wingless
Bird on your shoulder
What can you write

The bitterness is still rising in the old mines
The fist is coming out of the egg
The thermometers out of the mouths of the corpses

At a certain height
The tails of the kites for a moment are
Covered with footsteps

Whatever I have to do has not yet begun

## BREAD AT MIDNIGHT

The judges have chains in their sleeves
To get where they are they have
Studied many flies
They drag their voices up a long hill
Announcing It is over

Well now that it is over
I remember my homeland the mountains of chaff

And hands hands deaf as starfish fetching
The bread still frozen
To the tables


## CAESAR

My shoes are almost dead
And as I wait at the doors of ice
I hear the cry go up for him Caesar Caesar

But when I look out the window I see only the flatlands
And the slow vanishing of the windmills
The centuries draining the deep fields

Yet this is still my country
The thug on duty says What would you change
He looks at his watch he lifts
Emptiness out of the vases
And holds it up to examine

So it is evening
With the rain starting to fall forever

One by one he calls night out of the teeth
And at last I take up
My duty

Wheeling the president past banks of flowers
Past the feet of empty stairs
Hoping he's dead

PIECES FOR OTHER LIVES

I

Encouragement meant nothing

Inside it
The miners would continue to
Crawl out of their dark bodies
Extending the darkness making
It hollow
And how could they be rightly paid

Darkness gathered on the money
It lived in the dies the miners pursued it what
Was their reward

Some might bring flowers saying Nothing can last
Some anyway
Held out their whole lives in their glass hands

Sweeter than men till past the time
Some with a pure light burned but over
Their heads even theirs
Soot wrote on the ceiling
An unknown word

Shutting your eyes from the spectacle you
Saw not darkness but
Nothing

On which doors were opening

II

All that time with nothing to do
In that granite shed
The clinic by the rainy sea

While the doctor snake turned himself on at doors
In other rooms to study
Your life a small animal dying in a bottle

Out of what could be stolen and hidden you contrived
This model of the blood
A map in lost tubing and dead joints and you
Pointed out its comical story

It begins here it swells it goes along
It comes to the man sitting talking to a stick
Which he thinks is his dog or his wife
It comes to the river unwinding the stones
It takes up a thread it comes to the tailor saying
Thank you to his needle

Over and over here is the needle

It passes through his
One seam it comes to the door which is not shown

But which anyway is standing open
And beyond it there is

Salt water in unknown quantities

III

At one stroke out of the ruin
All the watches went out and
The eyes disappeared like martins into their nests

I woke to the slamming of doors and got up naked
The old wind vanished and vanished but was still there
Everyone but the cold was gone for good

And the carol of the miners had just ended


THE MOTHS


It is cold here
In the steel grass
At the foot of the invisible statue
Made by the incurables and called
Justice

At a great distance
An audience of rubber tombstones is watching
The skulls of
The leaders
Strung on the same worm

Darkness moves up the nail

And I am returning to a night long since past
In which the rain is falling and
A crying comes from the stations
And near at hand a voice a woman's
In a jug under the wind
Is trying to sing

No one has shown her
Any statue and
The music keeps rising through her
Almost beginning and
The moths
Lie in the black grass waiting


WHENEVER I GO THERE


Whenever I go there everything is changed

The stamps on the bandages the titles
Of the professors of water

The portrait of Glare the reasons for
The white mourning

In new rocks new insects are sitting
With the lights off
And once more I remember that the beginning

Is broken

No wonder the addresses are torn

To which I make my way eating the silence of animals
Offering snow to the darkness

Today belongs to few and tomorrow to no one

WISH

The star in my
Hand is falling

All the uniforms know what's no use

May I bow to Necessity not
To her hirelings


THE WAVE

I inhabited the wake of a long wave

As we sank it continued to rush past me
I knew where it had been
The light was full of salt and the air
Was heavy with crying for where the wave had come from
And why

It had brought them
From faces that soon were nothing but rain

Over the photographs they carried with them
The white forests
Grew impenetrable but as for themselves
They felt the sand slide from
Their roots of water

The harbors with outstretched arms retreated along
Glass corridors then
Were gone then their shadows were gone then the
Corridors were gone

Envelopes came each enfolding a little chalk
I inhabited the place where they opened them

I inhabited the sound of hope walking on water
Losing its way in the
Crowd so many footfalls of snow

I inhabit the sound of their pens on boxes
Writing to the dead in
Languages
I inhabit their wrappings sending back darkness
And the sinking of their voices entering
Nowhere as the wave passes

And asking where next as it breaks


## NEWS OF THE ASSASSIN


The clock strikes one one one
Through the window in a line pass
The bees whose flower is death

Why the morning smelled of honey

Already how long it is since the harvest
The dead animal fallen all the same way

On the stroke the wheels recall
That they are water
An empty window has overtaken me

After the bees comes the smell of cigars
In the lobby of darkness

APRIL

When we have gone the stone will stop singing

April April
Sinks through the sand of names

Days to come
With no stars hidden in them

You that can wait being there

You that lose nothing
Know nothing


THE GODS

If I have complained I hope I have done with it

I take no pride in circumstances but there are
Occupations
My blind neighbor has required of me
A description of darkness
And I begin I begin but

All day I keep hearing the fighting in the valley
The blows falling as rice and
With what cause
After these centuries gone and they had
Each their mourning for each of them grief
In hueless ribbons hung on walls
That fell
Their moment

Here in the future continues to find me
Till night wells up through the earth

I
Am all that became of them
Clearly all is lost

The gods are what has failed to become of us
Now it is over we do not speak

Now the moment has gone it is dark
What is man that he should be infinite
The music of a deaf planet
The one note
Continues clearly this is

The other world
These strewn rocks belong to the wind
If it could use them

## THE RIVER OF BEES

In a dream I returned to the river of bees
Five orange trees by the bridge and
Beside two mills my house
Into whose courtyard a blind man followed
The goats and stood singing
Of what was older

Soon it will be fifteen years

He was old he will have fallen into his eyes

I took my eyes
A long way to the calendars

Room after room asking how shall I live

One of the ends is made of streets
One man processions carry through it
Empty bottles their
Image of hope
It was offered to me by name

Once once and once
In the same city I was born
Asking what shall I say

He will have fallen into his mouth
Men think they are better than grass

I return to his voice rising like a forkful of hay

He was old he is not real nothing is real
Nor the noise of death drawing water

We are the echo of the future

On the door it says what to do to survive
But we were not born to survive
Only to live


## THE WIDOW


How easily the ripe grain
Leaves the husk
At the simple turning of the planet

There is no season
That requires us

Masters of forgetting
Threading the eyeless rocks with
A narrow light

In which ciphers wake and evil
Gets itself the face of the norm
And contrives cities

The Widow rises under our fingernails
In this sky we were born we are born

And you weep wishing you were numbers
You multiply you cannot be found
You grieve
Not that heaven does not exist but
That it exists without us

You confide
In images in things that can be
Represented which is their dimension you
Require them you say This
Is real and you do not fall down and moan

Not seeing the irony in the air

Everything that does not need you is real

The Widow does not
Hear you and your cry is numberless

This is the waking landscape
Dream after dream after dream walking away through it
Invisible invisible invisible

## LOOKING EAST AT NIGHT

Death
White hand
The moths fly at in the darkness

I took you for the moon rising

Whose light then
Do you reflect

As though it came out of the roots of things
This harvest pallor in which

I have no shadow but myself


## THE CHILD

Sometimes it is inconceivable that I should be the age I am
Almost always it is at a dry point in the afternoon
I cannot remember what
I am waiting for and in my astonishment I
Can hear the blood crawling over the plains
Hurrying on to arrive before dark
I try to remember my faults to make sure
One after the other but it is never
Satisfactory the list is never complete

At times night occurs to me so that I think I have been
Struck from behind I remain perfectly
Still feigning death listening for the

Assailant perhaps at last
I even sleep a little for later I have moved
I open my eyes the lanternfish have gone home in darkness
On all sides the silence is unharmed
I remember but I feel no bruise

Then there are the stories and after a while I think something
Else must connect them besides just this me
I regard myself starting the search turning
Corners in remembered metropoli
I pass skins withering in gardens that I see now
Are not familiar
And I have lost even the thread I thought I had

If I could be consistent even in destitution
The world would be revealed
While I can I try to repeat what I believe
Creatures spirits not this posture
I do not believe in knowledge as we know it
But I forget

This silence coming at intervals out of the shell of names
It must be all one person really coming at
Different hours for the same thing
If I could learn the word for yes it could teach me questions
I would see that it was itself every time and I would
Remember to say take it up like a hand
And go with it this is at last
Yourself

The child that will lead you

# A DEBT

I come on the debt again this day in November

It is raining into the yellow trees
The night kept raising white birds
The fowls of darkness entering winter
But I think of you seldom
You lost nothing you need entering death

I tell you the basket has woven itself over you
If there was grief it was in pencil on a wall
At no time had I asked you for anything

What did you take from me that I still owe you

Each time it is
A blind man opening his eyes

It is a true debt it can never be paid
How have you helped me
Is it with speech you that combed out your voice till the ends bled
Is it with hearing with waking of any kind
You in the wet veil that you chose it is not with memory
Not with sight of any kind not
Yet

It is a true debt it is mine alone
It is nameless
It rises from poverty
It goes out from me into the trees
Night falls

It follows a death like a candle
But the death is not yours

## THE PLASTER

How unlike you
To have left the best of your writings here
Behind the plaster where they were never to be found
These stanzas of long lines into which the Welsh words
Had been flung like planks from a rough sea
How will I

Ever know now how much was not like you
And what else was committed to paper here
On the dark burst sofa where you would later die
Its back has left a white mark on the white wall and above that
Five and a half indistinct squares of daylight
Like pages in water
Slide across the blind plaster

Into which you slipped the creased writings as into a mail slot
In a shroud

This is now the house of the rain that falls from death
The sky is moving its things in from under the trees
In silence
As it must have started to do even then
There is still a pile of dirty toys and rags
In the corner where they found the children
Rolled in sleep

Other writings
Must be dissolving in the roof
Twitching black edges in cracks of the wet fireplaces
Stuck to shelves in the filthy pantry
Never to be found
What is like you now

Who were haunted all your life by the best of you
Hiding in your death

## IN AUTUMN

The extinct animals are still looking for home
Their eyes full of cotton

Now they will
Never arrive

The stars are like that

Moving on without memory
Without having been near turning elsewhere climbing
Nothing the wall

The hours their shadows

The lights are going on in the leaves nothing to do with evening

Those are cities
Where I had hoped to live


## CROWS ON THE NORTH SLOPE

When the Gentle were dead these inherited their coats
Now they gather in late autumn and quarrel over the air
Demanding something for their shadows that are naked
And silent and learning

# NEW MOON IN NOVEMBER

I have been watching crows and now it is dark
Together they led night into the creaking oaks
Under them I hear the dry leaves walking
That blind man
Gathering their feathers before winter
By the dim road that the wind will take
And the cold
And the note of the trumpet


# DECEMBER NIGHT

The cold slope is standing in darkness
But the south of the trees is dry to the touch

The heavy limbs climb into the moonlight bearing feathers
I came to watch these
White plants older at night
The oldest
Come first to the ruins

And I hear magpies kept awake by the moon
The water flows through its
Own fingers without end

Tonight once more
I find a single prayer and it is not for men

## AFTER THE SOLSTICE

Under the east cliff the spring flows into the snow

The bird tracks end like calendars

At noon white hair
Is caught in the thorns of the abandoned vineyard
Here the sky passed

The old are buried all down the slope
Except the wrists and the ancient
Message *We are with no one*

At midnight we raise their wine to tomorrow


## DECEMBER AMONG THE VANISHED

The old snow gets up and moves taking its
Birds with it

The beasts hide in the knitted walls
From the winter that lipless man
Hinges echo but nothing opens

A silence before this one
Has left its broken huts facing the pastures
Through their stone roofs the snow
And the darkness walk down

In one of them I sit with a dead shepherd
And watch his lambs

## GLIMPSE OF THE ICE

I am sure now
A light under the skin coming nearer
Bringing snow
Then at nightfall a moth has thawed out and is
Dripping against the glass
I wonder if death will be silent after all
Or a cry frozen in another age

## THE COLD BEFORE THE MOONRISE

It is too simple to turn to the sound
Of frost stirring among its
Stars like an animal asleep
In the winter night
And say I was born far from home
If there is a place where this is the language may
It be my country

## EARLY JANUARY

A year has come to us as though out of hiding
It has arrived from an unknown distance
From beyond the visions of the old
Everyone waited for it by the wrong roads
And it is hard for us now to be sure it is here
A stranger to nothing
In our hiding places

# THE ROOM

I think all this is somewhere in myself
The cold room unlit before dawn
Containing a stillness such as attends death
And from a corner the sounds of a small bird trying
From time to time to fly a few beats in the dark
You would say it was dying it is immortal


# DUSK IN WINTER

The sun sets in the cold without friends
Without reproaches after all it has done for us
It goes down believing in nothing
When it has gone I hear the stream running after it
It has brought its flute it is a long way


# A SCALE IN MAY

Now all my teachers are dead except silence
I am trying to read what the five poplars are writing
On the void

———

Of all the beasts to man alone death brings justice
But I desire
To kneel in a doorway empty except for the song

———

Who made time provided also its fools
Strapped in watches and with ballots for their choices
Crossing the frontiers of invisible kingdoms

———

To succeed consider what is as though it were past
Deem yourself inevitable and take credit for it
If you find you no longer believe enlarge the temple

———

Through the day the nameless stars keep passing the door
That have come all that way out of death
Without questions

———

The walls of light shudder and an owl wakes in the heart
I cannot call upon words
The sun goes away to set elsewhere

———

Before nightfall colorless petals blow under the door
And the shadows
Recall their ancestors in the house beyond death

———

At the end of its procession through the stone
Falling
The water remembers to laugh


EVENING


I am strange here and often I am still trying
To finish something as the light is going
Occasionally as just now I think I see
Off to one side something passing at that time
Along the herded walls under the walnut trees
And I look up but it is only
Evening again the old hat without a head
How long will it be till he speaks when he passes

## THE DREAM AGAIN

I take the road that bears leaves in the mountains
I grow hard to see then I vanish entirely
On the peaks it is summer


## HOW WE ARE SPARED

At midsummer before dawn an orange light returns to the mountains
Like a great weight and the small birds cry out
And bear it up


## THE DRAGONFLY

Hoeing the bean field here are the dragonfly's wings
From this spot the wheat once signaled
With lights *It is all here*
With these feet on it
My own
And the hoe in my shadow


## PROVISION

All morning with dry instruments
The field repeats the sound
Of rain
From memory
And in the wall

The dead increase their invisible honey
It is August
The flocks are beginning to form
I will take with me the emptiness of my hands
What you do not have you find everywhere


## THE HERDS


Climbing northward
At dusk when the horizon rose like a hand I would turn aside
Before dark I would stop by the stream falling through black ice
And once more celebrate our distance from men

As I lay among stones high in the starless night
Out of the many hoof tracks the sounds of herds
Would begin to reach me again
Above them their ancient sun skating far off

Sleeping by the glass mountain
I would watch the flocks of light grazing
And the water preparing its descent
To the first dead


## THE MOURNER


On the south terraces of the glass palace
That has no bells
My hoe clacks in the bean rows
In the cool of the morning

At her hour
The mourner approaches on her way to the gate

A small old woman an aunt in the world
Without nephews or nieces
Her black straw hat shining like water
Floats back and forth climbing
Along the glass walls of the terraces
Bearing its purple wax rose

We nod as she passes slowly toward the palace
Her soft face with its tiny wattle flushed salmon
I hear her small soles receding
And remember the sound of the snow at night
Brushing the glass towers
In the time of the living


## FOR THE ANNIVERSARY OF MY DEATH


Every year without knowing it I have passed the day
When the last fires will wave to me
And the silence will set out
Tireless traveler
Like the beam of a lightless star

Then I will no longer
Find myself in life as in a strange garment
Surprised at the earth
And the love of one woman
And then shamelessness of men
As today writing after three days of rain
Hearing the wren sing and the falling cease
And bowing not knowing to what

DIVINITIES

Having crowded once onto the threshold of mortality
And not been chosen
There is no freedom such as theirs
That have no beginning

The air itself is their memory
A domain they cannot inhabit
But from which they are never absent

*What are you* they say *that simply exist*
And the heavens and the earth bow to them
Looking up from their choices
Perishing

All day and all night
Everything that is mistaken worships them
Even the dead sing them an unending hymn


THE DRY STONE MASON

The mason is dead the gentle drunk
Master of dry walls
What he made of his years crosses the slopes without wavering
Upright but nameless
Ignorant in the new winter
Rubbed by running sheep
But the age of mortar has come to him

Bottles are waiting like fallen shrines
Under different trees in the rain
And stones drip where his hands left them

Leaning slightly inwards
His thirst is past

As he had no wife
The neighbors found where he kept his suit
A man with no family they sat with him
When he was carried through them they stood by their own dead
And they have buried him among the graves of the stones


## IN THE WINTER OF MY THIRTY-EIGHTH YEAR


It sounds unconvincing to say *When I was young*
Though I have long wondered what it would be like
To be me now
No older at all it seems from here
As far from myself as ever

Waking in fog and rain and seeing nothing
I imagine all the clocks have died in the night
Now no one is looking I could choose my age
It would be younger I suppose so I am older
It is there at hand I could take it
Except for the things I think I would do differently
They keep coming between they are what I am
They have taught me little I did not know when I was young

There is nothing wrong with my age now probably
It is how I have come to it
Like a thing I kept putting off as I did my youth

There is nothing the matter with speech
Just because it lent itself
To my uses

Of course there is nothing the matter with the stars
It is my emptiness among them
While they drift farther away in the invisible morning


WHEN YOU GO AWAY


When you go away the wind clicks around to the north
The painters work all day but at sundown the paint falls
Showing the black walls
The clock goes back to striking the same hour
That has no place in the years

And at night wrapped in the bed of ashes
In one breath I wake
It is the time when the beards of the dead get their growth
I remember that I am falling
That I am the reason
And that my words are the garment of what I shall never be
Like the tucked sleeve of a one-armed boy


THE ASIANS DYING


When the forests have been destroyed their darkness remains
The ash the great walker follows the possessors
Forever
Nothing they will come to is real
Nor for long
Over the watercourses
Like ducks in the time of the ducks
The ghosts of the villages trail in the sky
Making a new twilight

Rain falls into the open eyes of the dead
Again again with its pointless sound
When the moon finds them they are the color of everything

The nights disappear like bruises but nothing is healed
The dead go away like bruises
The blood vanishes into the poisoned farmlands
Pain the horizon
Remains
Overhead the seasons rock
They are paper bells
Calling to nothing living

The possessors move everywhere under Death their star
Like columns of smoke they advance into the shadows
Like thin flames with no light
They with no past
And fire their only future

WHEN THE WAR IS OVER

When the war is over
We will be proud of course the air will be
Good for breathing at last
The water will have been improved the salmon
And the silence of heaven will migrate more perfectly
The dead will think the living are worth it we will know
Who we are
And we will all enlist again

# PEASANT

*His Prayer To The Powers Of This World*

All those years that you ate and changed
And grew under my picture
You saw nothing
It was only when I began to appear
That you said I must vanish

What could I do I thought things were real
Cruel and wise
And came and went in their names
I thought I would wait I was shrewder but you
Were dealing in something else

You were always embarrassed by what fed you
And made distances faster
Than you destroyed them
It bewitched my dreams
Like magazines I took out with the sheep
That helped to empty the hours
I tried to despise you for what you did not
Need to be able to do
If I could do it
Maybe I could have done without you

My contempt for you
You named ignorance and my admiration for you
Servility
When they were among the few things we had in common
Your trash and your poses were what I most appreciated
Just as you did

And the way you were free
Of me
But I fought in your wars
The way you could decide that things were not
And they died

The way you had reasons
Good enough for your time

When God was dying you bought him out
As you were in a position to do
Coming in the pale car through the mud and fresh dung
Unable to find the place though you had been there
Once at least before
Like the doctor
Without a moment to lose
I was somewhere
In the bargain

I was used to standing in the shade of the sky
A survivor
I had nothing you
Could use

I am taking my hands
Into the cleft wood assembled
In dry corners of abandoned barns
Beams being saved
For nothing broken doors pieces of carts
Other shadows have gone in there and
Wait
On hewn feet I follow the hopes of the owls
For a time I will
Drift down from the tool scars in a fine dust
Noticeably before rain in summer
And at the time of the first thaws
And at the sound of your frequent explosions
And when the roofs
Fall it will be a long while
Since anyone could still believe in me
Any more than if I were one of the
Immortals

It was you
That made the future
It was yours to take away
I see
Oh thousand gods
Only you are real
It is my shame that you did not
Make me
I am bringing up my children to be you


FOR A COMING EXTINCTION


Gray whale
Now that we are sending you to The End
That great god
Tell him
That we who follow you invented forgiveness
And forgive nothing

I write as though you could understand
And I could say it
One must always pretend something
Among the dying
When you have left the seas nodding on their stalks
Empty of you
Tell him that we were made
On another day

The bewilderment will diminish like an echo
Winding along your inner mountains
Unheard by us
And find its way out
Leaving behind it the future

Dead
And ours

When you will not see again
The whale calves trying the light
Consider what you will find in the black garden
And its court
The sea cows the Great Auks the gorillas
The irreplaceable hosts ranged countless
And foreordaining as stars
Our sacrifices

Join your word to theirs
Tell him
That it is we who are important


IN A CLEARING


The unnumbered herds flow like lichens
Along the darkness each carpet at its height
In silence
Herds without end
Without death
Nothing is before them nothing after
Among the hooves the hooves' brothers the shells
In a sea

Passing through senses
As through bright clearings surrounded with pain
Some of the animals
See souls moving in their word death
With its many tongues that no god could speak
That can describe
Nothing that cannot die

The word
Surrounds the souls
The hide they wear
Like a light in the light
And when it goes out they vanish

In the eyes of the herds there is only one light
They cherish it with the darkness it belongs to
They take their way through it nothing is
Before them and they leave it
A small place
Where dying a sun rises


AVOIDING NEWS BY THE RIVER


As the stars hide in the light before daybreak
Reed warblers hunt along the narrow stream
Trout rise to their shadows
Milky light flows through the branches
Fills with blood
Men will be waking

In an hour it will be summer
I dreamed that the heavens were eating the earth
Waking it is not so
Not the heavens
I am not ashamed of the wren's murders
Nor the badger's dinners
On which all worldly good depends
If I were not human I would not be ashamed of anything

## DEATH OF A FAVORITE BIRD

What was the matter with life on my shoulder
Age that I was wing delight
That you had to thresh out your breath in the spiked rafters
To the beat of rain
I have asked this question before it knows me it comes
Back to find me through the cold dreamless summer
And the barn full of black feathers


## FLY

I have been cruel to a fat pigeon
Because he would not fly
All he wanted was to live like a friendly old man

He had let himself become a wreck filthy and confiding
Wild for his food beating the cat off the garbage
Ignoring his mate perpetually snotty at the beak
Smelling waddling having to be
Carried up the ladder at night content

*Fly* I said throwing him into the air
But he would drop and run back expecting to be fed
I said it again and again throwing him up
As he got worse
He let himself be picked up every time
Until I found him in the dovecote dead
Of the needless efforts

So that is what I am

Pondering his eye that could not
Conceive that I was a creature to run from

I who have always believed too much in words


## THE FINDING OF REASONS


Every memory is abandoned
As waves leave their shapes
The houses stand in tears as the sun rises

Even Pain
That is a god to the senses
Can be forgotten
Until he returns in the flashing garments
And the senses themselves
Are to be taken away like clothing
After a sickness

Proud of their secrets as the dead
Our uses forsake us
That have been betrayed
They follow tracks that lead before and after
And over water
The prints cross us
When they have gone we find reasons

As though to relinquish a journey
Were to arrive
As though we had not been made
Of distances that would not again be ours
As though our feet would come to us once more
Of themselves freely

To us
Their forgotten masters

To listen to the announcements you would think
The triumph
Were ours
As the string of the great kite Sapiens
Cuts our palms
Along predestined places
Leaving us
Leaving
While we find reasons


## COME BACK


You came back to us in a dream and we were not here
In a light dress laughing you ran down the slope
To the door
And knocked for a long time thinking it strange

Oh come back we were watching all the time
With the delight choking us and the piled
Grief scrambling like guilt to leave us
At the sight of you
Looking well
And besides our questions our news
All of it paralyzed until you were gone

Is it the same way there

## WATCHERS

The mowers begin
And after this morning the fox
Will no longer glide close to the house in full day
When a breath stirs the wheat
Leaving his sounds waiting at a distance
Under a few trees

And lie out
Watching from the nodding light the birds on the roofs
The noon sleep

Perhaps nothing
For some time will cross the new size of the stubble fields
In the light
And watch us
But the day itself coming alone
From the woods with its hunger
Today a tall man saying nothing but taking notes
Tomorrow a colorless woman standing
With her reproach and her bony children
Before rain


## MY BROTHERS THE SILENT

My brothers the silent
At any hour finding
Blackness to stand in like cold stars my brothers
The invisible
What an uncharitable family
My brothers shepherds older than birth
What are you afraid of since I was born
I cannot touch the inheritance what is my age to you

I am not sure I would know what to ask for
I do not know what my hands are for
I do not know what my wars are deciding
I cannot make up my mind
I have the pitiless blood and the remote gaze of our lineage
But I will leave nothing to strangers
Look how I am attached to the ends of things
Even your sheep our sheep
When I meet them on the roads raise toward me
Their clear eyes unknowable as days
And if they see me do not recognize me do not
Believe in me


## IN ONE OF THE RETREATS OF MORNING


There are still bits of night like closed eyes in the walls
And at their feet the large brotherhood of broken stones
Is still asleep
I go quietly along the edge of their garden
Looking at the few things they grow for themselves


## LOOKING FOR MUSHROOMS AT SUNRISE

*for Jean and Bill Arrowsmith*

When it is not yet day
I am walking on centuries of dead chestnut leaves
In a place without grief
Though the oriole
Out of another life warns me
That I am awake

In the dark while the rain fell
The gold chanterelles pushed through a sleep that was not mine

Waking me
So that I came up the mountain to find them

Where they appear it seems I have been before
I recognize their haunts as though remembering
Another life

Where else am I walking even now
Looking for me

# THE

# CARRIER OF

# LADDERS

## (1970)

PLANE

We hurtle forward and seem to rise

I imagine the deities come and go
without departures

and with my mind infinitely divided and hopeless
like a stockyard seen from above
and my will like a withered body muffled
in qualifications until it has no shape
I bleed in my place

where is no
vision of the essential nakedness of the gods
nor of that
nakedness the seamless garment of heaven

nor of any other
nakedness

Here
is the air

and your tears flowing on the wings of the plane
where once again I cannot
reach to stop them

and they fall away behind
going with me

# TEACHERS

Pain is in this dark room like many speakers
of a costly set though mute
as here the needle and the turning

the night lengthens it is winter
a new year

what I live for I can seldom believe in
who I love I cannot go to
what I hope is always divided

but I say to myself you are not a child now
if the night is long remember your unimportance
sleep

then toward morning I dream of the first words
of books of voyages
sure tellings that did not start by justifying

yet at one time it seems
had taught me


# THE OWL

These woods are one of my great lies
I pretend
oh I have always pretended they
were mine
I stumble among
the smaller lies
as this night falls and
of my pretenses likewise

some
and your voice
begins

who need no hope to
hunt here who
love me
I retreat before
your question as before my own
through old branches who
am I hiding
what creature in the bowels quaking
that should not be raised
against the night
crying its truth at last

No I who
love you
find while I can some light to crawl into
maybe
I will never answer
though your dark lasts as my own does
and your voice in it without hope
or need of it
calling what I call calling
me me *You*
*who are never there*

## THE DIFFERENT STARS

I could never have come to the present without you
remember that
from whatever stage we may again
watch it appear

with its lines clear
pain
having gone from there

so that we may well wonder
looking back on us here what tormented us
what great difficulty invisible
in a time that by then looks simple
and is irrevocable

pain having come from there
my love
I tend to think of division as the only evil
when perhaps it is merely my own

that unties
one day the veins one the arteries
that prizes less
as it receives than as it loses
that breaks the compasses
cannot be led or followed
cannot choose what to carry
into grief
even
unbinds will unbind
unbinds our hands
pages of the same story

what is it
they say can turn even this into wisdom

and what is wisdom if it is not
now
in the loss that has not left this place

oh if we knew
if we knew what we needed if we even knew
the stars would look to us to guide them


THE DEAD HIVE


The year still a child
but its sunlight
climbing for the first time in the poplars
pretending to be older
and the green has been lit in the east-sloping
pastures guarded
by nurses of shadow
a ghost has risen out of the earth
the unnamed warmth
saved for now

in the silence
one note is missing
I see
you nowhere I hear you nowhere
I climb to your hall you are nowhere
the flowers nod in the sun
like the blind
I knock
from the arcade of your portal
a fly steps out

I open the roof
I and the light
this is how it looks later

the city the dance the care
the darkness
the moment
one at a time
that is each one alone

as she
turns aside
obeying as always
and the accomplished limbs begin
welcoming
what does not move
and the eyes
go as far as they can
and wait

at the place where no one they know
can fail them


## THE MOUNTAINS


There are days when I think the future sets
beyond the mountains
then I lay me down
in fear of departures

and a heavy
net drops on me when I wake
far
far in the night
borne on
and the whole air
around me crying for you
even
when you are still there

and a dog barking
beyond it
at an unknown distance

on and on


## THE BRIDGES


Nothing but me is moving
on these bridges
as I always knew it would be
see moving on each of the bridges
only me

and everything that we have known
even the friends
lined up in the silent iron railings
back and forth
I pass like a stick on palings

the echo
rises from the marbled river
the light from the blank clocks crackles
like an empty film
where
are we living now
on which side which side
and will you be there

## THE HANDS

*. . . Ma non è cosa in terra*
*Che ti somigli . . .*
LEOPARDI

I have seen them when there was
nothing else
small swollen flames lighting my way at
corners
where they have waited for
me

cut off from
everything they have made their way to me
one more day one more night leading
their blood and I wake
to find them lying at home
with my own

like a bird lying in its wings
a stunned
bird till they stir and
break
open cradling a heart not theirs
not mine
and I bend to hear who is beating

## DO NOT DIE

In each world they may put us
farther apart
do not die
as this world is made I might
live forever

# WORDS FROM A TOTEM ANIMAL

Distance
is where we were
but empty of us and ahead of
me lying out in the rushes thinking
even the nights cannot come back to their hill
any time

————

I would rather the wind came from outside
from mountains anywhere
from the stars from other
worlds even as
cold as it is this
ghost of mine passing
through me

————

I know your silence
and the repetition
like that of a word in the ear of death
teaching
itself
itself
that is the sound of my running
the plea
plea that it makes
which you will never hear
oh god of beginnings
immortal

————

I might have been right
not who I am
but all right
among the walls among the reasons
not even waiting
not seen
but now I am out in my feet

and they on their way
the old trees jump up again and again
strangers
there are no names for the rivers
for the days for the nights
I am who I am
oh lord cold as the thoughts of birds
and everyone can see me

———

Caught again and held again
again I am not a blessing
they bring me
names
that would fit anything
they bring them to me
they bring me hopes
all day I turn
making ropes
helping

———

My eyes are waiting for me
in the dusk
they are still closed
they have been waiting a long time
and I am feeling my way toward them

———

I am going up stream
taking to the water from time to time
my marks dry off the stones before morning
the dark surface
strokes the night
above its way
There are no stars
there is no grief
I will never arrive
I stumble when I remember how it was
with one foot
one foot still in a name

I can turn myself toward the other joys and their lights
but not find them
I can put my words into the mouths
of spirits
but they will not say them
I can run all night and win
and win

———

Dead leaves crushed grasses fallen limbs
the world is full of prayers
arrived at from
afterwards
a voice full of breaking
heard from afterwards
through all
the length of the night

———

I am never all of me
unto myself
and sometimes I go slowly
knowing that a sound one sound
is following me from world
to world
and that I die each time
before it reaches me

———

When I stop I am alone
at night sometimes it is almost good
as though I were almost there
sometimes then I see there is
in a bush beside me the same question
why are you
on this way
I said I will ask the stars
why are you falling and they answered
which of us

———

I dreamed I had no nails
no hair
I had lost one of the senses
not sure which
the soles peeled from my feet and
drifted away
clouds
It's all one
feet
stay mine
hold the world lightly

———

Stars even you
have been used
but not you
silence
blessing
calling me when I am lost

———

Maybe I will come
to where I am one
and find
I have been waiting there
as a new
year finds the song of the nuthatch

———

Send me out into another life
lord because this one is growing faint
I do not think it goes all the way

## ANIMULA

Look soul
soul
barefoot presence
through whom blood falls as through
a water clock
and tears rise before they wake
I will take you

at last to
where the wind stops
by the river we
know
by that same water
and the nights are not separate
remember


## QUINCE

The gentle quince blossoms open
they have no first youth
they look down on me
knowing me well
some place I had left

# THE JUDGMENT OF PARIS

*for Anthony Hecht*

Long afterwards
the intelligent could deduce what had been offered
and not recognized
and they suggest that bitterness should be confined
to the fact that the gods chose for their arbiter
a mind and character so ordinary
albeit a prince

and brought up as a shepherd
a calling he must have liked
for he had returned to it

when they stood before him
the three
naked feminine deathless
and he realized that he was clothed
in nothing but mortality
the strap of his quiver of arrows crossing
between his nipples
making it seem stranger

and he knew he must choose
and on that day

the one with the gray eyes spoke first
and whatever she said he kept
thinking he remembered
but remembered it woven with confusion and fear
the two faces that he called father
the first sight of the palace
where the brothers were strangers
and the dogs watched him and refused to know him
she made everything clear she was dazzling she
offered it to him
to have for his own but what he saw

was the scorn above her eyes
and her words of which he understood few
all said to him *Take wisdom*
*take power*
*you will forget anyway*

the one with the dark eyes spoke
and everything she said
he imagined he had once wished for
but in confusion and cowardice
the crown
of his father the crowns the crowns bowing to him
his name everywhere like grass
only he and the sea
triumphant
she made everything sound possible she was
dazzling she offered it to him
to hold high but what he saw
was the cruelty around her mouth
and her words of which he understood more
all said to him *Take pride*
*take glory*
*you will suffer anyway*

the third one the color of whose eyes
later he could not remember
spoke last and slowly and
of desire and it was his
though up until then he had been
happy with his river nymph
here was his mind
filled utterly with one girl gathering
yellow flowers
and no one like her
the words
made everything seem present
almost present
present

they said to him *Take*
*her*
*you will lose her anyway*

it was only when he reached out to the voice
as though he could take the speaker
herself
that his hand filled with
something to give
but to give to only one of the three
an apple as it is told
discord itself in a single fruit its skin
already carved
*To the fairest*

then a mason working above the gates of Troy
in the sunlight thought he felt the stone
shiver

in the quiver on Paris's back the head
of the arrow for Achilles' heel
smiled in its sleep

and Helen stepped from the palace to gather
as she would do every day in that season
from the grove the yellow ray flowers tall
as herself

whose roots are said to dispel pain

# EDOUARD

Edouard shall we leave
tomorrow
for Verdun again
shall we set out for the great days
and never be the same
never

time
is what is left
shall we start
this time in the spring
and they lead your cows out
next week to sell at the fair
and the brambles learn to scribble
over the first field

Edouard shall we have gone
when the leaves come out
but before the heat
slows the grand marches
days like those
the heights and the dying
at thy right hand
sound a long horn
and here the bright handles
will fog over
things will break and stay broken
in the keeping of women
the sheep get lost
the barns
burn unconsoled in the darkness

Edouard what would you have given
not to go
sitting last night in by the fire

again
but shall we be the same
tomorrow night shall we not have gone
leaving the faces and nightingales
As you know we will live
and what never comes back will be
you and me


## NOT THESE HILLS


Not these hills
are in my tongue
though I inquire of them again
which then
with their later season
on whose slopes my voice stirs
shining root
stream carrying small lights
to where one echo
waits

spring here
I am shown to me
as flies waking in the south walls
emerging from darkness one
at a time
dark
then gone
with nothing between them
but the sun

# THE PIPER

It is twenty years
since I first looked for words
for me now
whose wisdom or something would stay me
I chose to
trouble myself about the onset
of this
it was remote it was grievous
it is true I was still a child

I was older then
than I hope ever to be again
that summer sweating in the attic
in the foreign country
high above the piper but hearing him
once
and never moving from my book
and the narrow
house full of pregnant women
floor above floor
waiting
in that city
where the sun was the one bell

It has taken me till now
to be able to say
even this
it has taken me this long
to know what I cannot say
where it begins
like the names of the hungry

Beginning
I am here
please
be ready to teach me
I am almost ready to learn


## THE LAKE


Did you exist
ever

our clouds separated while it was still dark
then I could not sleep the sleep of a child
I got up to look for you
bringing my silence
all of it

no father in the house at least

I got my boat
that we had saved for each other
a white creature my
wise elder
You rustled as it slid
from shore

I lay there
looking down while the mist was torn
looking down
where
was the Indian village
said to be drowned there

one glimpse and I would have hung
fixed in its sky

when the dawn was gone
and the morning star
and the wind
and the sun
and the calling around you


## THE CHURCH


High walls
pale brick like Babylon
above the cliff face
the house
of the lord

at the single window
up in the back
toward the river
the eyes I left
as a child there

everything gone now
the walls are down
the altar
only I am still standing
on the weedy rock in the wind
there is no building here

there are my hands
that have known between them
the bride
and call to her
wherever she is not wherever
she is *Hand*

*hand*

# A CALM IN APRIL

Early mist
mountains like a rack of dishes
in a house I love
far mountains
last night the stars for a while
stopped trembling
and this morning the light will speak to me
of what concerns me


# THE BIRDS ON THE MORNING OF GOING

If I can say yes I
must say it to this
and now
trying to remember what the present
can bless with
which I know

from all other ages how little has come to me
that is breath
and nothing that is you

now I can see
I have been carrying this
fear
a blue thing
the length of my life asking *Is this*
*its place*
bringing it here

to the singing
of these brightening birds

they are neither dead nor unborn

a life opens it opens it is
breaking
does it find occasions for
every grief of its childhood
before it will have
done

oh my love here even the night turns back

## ENVOY FROM D'AUBIGNÉ

Go book

go
now I will let you
I open the grave
live
I will die for us both

go but come again if you can
and feed me in prison

if they ask you why
you do not boast of me
tell them as they
have forgotten
truth habitually
gives birth in private

Go without ornament
without showy garment
if there is in you any
joy

may the good find it

for the others be
a glass broken in their mouths

Child
how will you
survive with nothing but your virtue
to draw around you
when they shout Die die

who have been frightened before
the many

I think of all I wrote in my time
dew
and I am standing in dry air

Here are what flowers there are
and what hope
from my years

and the fire I carried with me

Book
burn what will not abide your light

When I consider the old ambitions
to be on many lips
meaning little there
it would be enough for me to know
who is writing this
and sleep knowing it

far from glory and its gibbets

and dream of those who drank at the icy fountain
and told the truth

ENCOUNTER


Name for a curtain at night
sister of some
unfueled flame

imperious
triumphant and unloved
how did you find the houses
from which now you emanate
in which someone has just

but no sound reaches the gate
here
though all the lights are burning


THE WELL


Under the stone sky the water
waits
with all its songs inside it
the immortal
it sang once
it will sing again
the days
walk across the stone in heaven
unseen as planets at noon
while the water
watches the same night

Echoes come in like swallows
calling to it

it answers without moving
but in echoes
not in its voice
they do not say what it is
only where

It is a city to which many travelers
came with clear minds
having left everything even
heaven
to sit in the dark praying as one silence
for the resurrection


LARK


In the hour that has no friends
above it
you become yourself
voice
black
star burning in cold heaven
speaking well of it
as it falls from you
upward

Fire
by day
with no country
where and at what height
can it begin
I the shadow
singing I
the light

# THE BLACK PLATEAU

The cows bring in the last light
the dogs praise them
one by one they proceed through the stone arch
on the chine of the hill
and their reflections in the little
cold darkening stream
and the man with the pole
then the night comes down to its roads
full of love for them

———

I go eating nothing so you will be one and clear
but then how could you drown
in this arid country of stone and dark dew
I shake you in your heavy sleep
then the sun comes
and I see you are one of the stones

———

Like a little smoke in the vault
light for going
before the dogs wake in the cracked barn
the owl has come in from his shift
the water in the stone basin has forgotten
where I touch the ashes they are cold
everything is in order

———

Kestrel and lark shimmer over the high stone
like two brothers who avoid each other
on the cliff corner I met the wind
a brother

———

Almost everything you look on great sun
has fallen into itself here
which it had climbed out of like prayers
shadows of clouds

and the clothes of old women blow over the barrens
one apple tree still blossoms for its own sake

————

The cold of the heights is not the cold of the valleys
the light moves like a wind
the figures are far away walking slowly
in little knots herding pieces of darkness
their faces remote as the plaster above deaths
in the villages

————

The upper window of a ruin
one of the old faces
many places near here
things grow old where nothing was ever a child

————

Oh blessed goat live goat blessed rat
and neither of you lost

————

There is still warmth in the goat sheds years afterwards
in the abandoned fountain a dead branch points
upwards
eaten out from inside as it appears to me
I know a new legend
this is the saint of the place his present form
another blessing in absence
when the last stone has fallen he will rise
from the water
and the butterflies will tell him what he needs to know
that happened while he was asleep

————

The beginnings and ends of days like the butts of arches
reach for roofs that have fallen
the sun up there was never enough
high in its light
the bird moves apart from his cry

## THE APPROACHES

The glittering rises in flocks
suddenly in the afternoon
and hangs
voiceless above the broken
houses
the cold in the doorways
and at the silent station
the hammers
out of hearts
laid out in rows in the grass

The water is asleep
as they say
everywhere
cold cold
and at night the sky
is in many
pieces in the dark
the stars set out
and leave their light

When I wake
I say I may never
get there but should get
closer and hear the sound
seeing figures I go toward them waving
they make off
birds
no one to guide me
afraid
to the warm ruins
Canaan
where the fighting is

# THE WHEELS OF THE TRAINS

They are there just the same
unnoticed for years
on dark tracks at the foot of their mountain

behind them holes in the hill
endless death of the sky
foreheads long unlit
illegibly inscribed

the cars
have been called into the air
an air that has gone
but these wait unmoved in their rust
row of suns
for another life

ahead of them
the tracks lead out through tall milkweed
untouched

for all my travels


## LACKAWANNA

Where you begin
in me
I have never seen
but I believe it now
rising dark
but clear

later when I lived where
you went past
already you were black
moving under gases by
red windows
obedient child
I shrank from you

on girders of your bridges
I ran
told to be afraid
obedient
the arches never touched you the running
shadow never
looked
the iron
and black ice never
stopped ringing under foot

terror
a truth
lived alone in the stained buildings
in the streets a smoke
an eyelid a clock
a black winter all year
like a dust
melting and freezing in silence

you flowed from under
and through the night the dead drifted down you
all the dead
what was found later no one
could recognize

told to be afraid
I wake black to the knees
so it has happened
I have set foot in you

both feet
Jordan
too long I was ashamed
at a distance


OTHER TRAVELERS TO THE RIVER


William Bartram how many
have appeared in their sleep
climbing like flames into
your eyes
and have stood gazing out over the sire of waters
with night behind them
in the east
The tall bank where you stood
would soon crumble
you would die before they were born
they would wake not remembering
and on the river
that same day
was bearing off its empty flower again
and overhead the sounds of the earth
danced naked
thinking no one could see them


THE TRAIL INTO KANSAS


The early wagons left no sign
no smoke betrays them
line pressed in the grass *we were here*
all night the sun bleeds in us
and the wound slows us in the daytime

will it heal
there

we few
late
we gave our names to each other to keep
wrapped in their old bells
the wrappings work loose
something eats them when we sleep and wake us
ringing

when day comes
shadows that were once ours and came back to look
stand up for a moment ahead of us
and then vanish
we know we are
watched but there is no danger
nothing that lives waits for us
nothing is eternal

we have been guided from scattered wombs
all the way here choosing choosing
which foot to put down
we are like wells moving
over the prairie
a blindness a hollow a cold source
will any be happy to see us
in the new home

WESTERN COUNTRY

Some days after so long even the sun
is foreign
I watch the exiles
their stride

stayed by their antique faith that no one
can die in exile
when all that is true is that death is not exile

Each no doubt knows a western country
half discovered
which he thinks is there because
he thinks he left it
and its names are still written in the sun
in his age and he knows them
but he will never tread their ground

At some distances I can no longer
sleep
my countrymen are more cruel than their stars
and I know what moves the long
files stretching into the mountains
each man with his gun
his feet
one finger's breadth off the ground


THE GARDENS OF ZUÑI


The one-armed explorer
could touch only half of the country
In the virgin half
the house fires give no more heat
than the stars
it has been so these many years
and there is no bleeding

He is long dead with his five fingers
and the sum of their touching
and the memory

of the other hand
his scout

that sent back no message
from where it had reached
with no lines in its palm
while he balanced
balanced
and groped on
for the virgin land

and found where it had been


HOMELAND


The sky goes on living it goes
on living the sky
with all the barbed wire of the west
in its veins
and the sun goes down
driving a stake
through the black heart of Andrew Jackson


FEBRUARY


Dawn that cares for nobody
comes home
to the glass cliffs
an expression
needing no face
the river flies under cold feathers

flies on
leaving its body
the black streets bare their veins
night
lives on in the uniforms
in the silence of the headlines
in the promises of triumph
in the colors of the flags
in a room of the heart
while the ends and the beginnings
are still guarded
by lines of doors
hand in hand
the dead guarding the invisible
each presenting its message
*I know nothing*
*learn of me*


## HUCKLEBERRY WOMAN


Foreign voice woman
of unnamed origins nothing
to do with what I was taught
at night when it was nobody's
you climbed the mountain in back of the house
the thorn bushes slept
in their words
before day you put on
the bent back like a hill
the hands at the berries

and I wake only to the crying
when the washtub has
fallen from your head and the alley
under the window is deep

in the spilled blue of far ranges
the rolling of small
starless skies and you turning
among them key
unlocking the presence
of the unlighted river
under the mountains

and I am borne with you on its
black stream
oh loss loss the grieving
feels its way upward
through daggers of stone
to stone
we let it go it
stays we share it
echoed by a wooden
coughing of oars in the dark
whether or not they are ours
we go with the sound


## LITTLE HORSE


You come from some other forest
do you
little horse
think how long I have known these
deep dead leaves
without meeting you

I belong to no one
I would have wished for you if I had known how
what a long time the place was empty
even in my sleep

and loving it as I did
I could not have told what was missing

what can I show you
I will not ask you if you will stay
or if you will come again
I will not try to hold you
I hope you will come with me to where I stand
often sleeping and waking
by the patient water
that has no father nor mother


THE PORT


The river is slow
and I knew I was late arriving but had no idea
how late
in the splintery fishing port silence
was waving from the nails
dry long since
the windows though rattling
were fixed in time and space
in a way that I am not nor ever was
and the boats were out of sight

all but one
by the wharf
full of water
with my rotted sea–clothes lashed to a piling
at its head
and a white note nailed there in a can
with white words
I was too late to read

when what I came to say is I have learned who we are

when what I came to say was
consider consider
our voices
through the salt

they waken in heads
in the deaths themselves

that was part of it

when what I came to say was
it is true that in
our language deaths are to be heard
at any moment through the talk
pacing their wooden rooms jarring
the dried flowers
but they have forgotten who they are
and our voices in their heads waken
childhoods in other tongues

but the whole town has gone to sea without a word
taking my voice


## PRESIDENTS


The president of shame has his own flag
the president of lies quotes the voice
of God
as last counted
the president of loyalty recommends
blindness to the blind
oh oh
applause like the heels of the hanged
he walks on eyes
until they break

then he rides
there is no president of grief
it is a kingdom
ancient absolute with no colors
its ruler is never seen
prayers look for him
also empty flags like skins
silence the messenger runs through the vast lands
with a black mouth
open
silence the climber falls from the cliffs
with a black mouth like
a call
there is only one subject
but he is repeated
tirelessly


THE FREE


So far from the murders
the ruts begin to bleed
but no one hears
our voices
above the sound of the reddening feet
they leave us the empty roads
they leave us
for companions for messengers
for signs
the autumn leaves
before the winter panes
we move among them
doubly invisible
like air touching the blind
and when we have gone they say we are with them forever

## THE PRINTS

Above white paths a bugle
will sound from the top of an unseen wall
and beds be empty as far as eye will reach
made up spotless
the shallow prints where each traveler carried
what he had

whiteness came back to the paths after each
footstep and the travelers
never met in the single files
who deepened the same
shadows

while the snow fell

## THE REMOVAL

*To the endless tribe*

I   *The Procession*

When we see
the houses again
we will know that we are asleep at last

when we see
tears on the road
and they are ourselves
we are awake
the tree has been cut
on which we were leaves
the day does not know us
the river where we cross does not taste salt

the soles of our feet are black stars
but ours is the theme
of the light

II   *The Homeless*

A clock keeps striking
and the echoes move in files
their faces
have been lost
flowers of salt
tongues from lost languages
doorways closed with pieces of night

III   *A Survivor*

The dust never settles
but through it tongue tongue comes walking
shuffling like breath
but the old speech
is still in its country
dead

IV   *The Crossing of the Removed*

At the bottom of the river
black ribbons cross under
and the water tries to soothe them
the mud tries to soothe them
the stones turn over and over trying
to comfort them
but they will not be healed
where the rims cut
and the shadows
sawed carrying
mourners
and some that had used horses
and had the harness

dropped it in half way over
on the far side the ribbons come out
invisible


v    *A Widow Is Taken*


I call leave me here
the smoke on the black path
was my children
I will not walk
from the house I warmed
but they carry me through the light
my blackening face
my red eyes
everywhere I leave
one white footprint
the trackers will follow us into the cold
the water is high
the boats have been stolen away
there are no shoes
and they pretend that I am a bride
on the way to a new house


v i    *The Reflection*


Passing a broken window
they see
into each of them the wedge of blackness
pounded
it is nothing
it splits them
loose hair
bare heels
at last they are gone
filing on in vacant rooms

# THE OLD ROOM

I am in the old room across from the synagogue
a dead chief hangs in the wallpaper
he is shrinking into the patch of sunlight
with its waves and nests and in the silence that follows
his death
the parade is forming again
with the streetcar for its band
it is forming I hear the shuffling the whispers
the choking then the grinding starts off
slowly as ice melting
they will pass by the house

closed ranks attached to the iron trolley
dragged on their backs
the black sleeves the fingers waving like banners
I am forbidden to look
but the faces are wrapped except for the eyes
darkness wells from the bandages
spreads
its loaves and fishes while on the curbs
the police the citizens
of all ages beat the muffled street with bars

what if I call *It is not me* will it stop
what if I raise an arm
to stop it
I raise an arm the whole arm stays white
dry as a beach
little winds play over it
a sunny and a pleasant place I hold it
out it leaves me it goes toward them
the man in charge is a friend of the family
he smiles when he sees it he takes its hand
he gives it its bar
it drops it

I am forbidden to look

I am in the old room across from the stone star
the moon is climbing in gauze
the street is empty
except for the dark liquid running
in the tracks of ice
trying to call
*Wait*
but the wires are taken up with the election
there is a poll at the corner I am not to go in
but I can look in the drugstore window
where the numbers of the dead change all night on the wall
what if I vote *It is not me* will they revive
I go in my father has voted for me
I say no I will vote in my own name
I vote and the number leaps again on the wall

I am in the old room across from the night
the long scream is about to blossom
that is rooted in flames
if I called *It is not me* would it reach
through the bells


## THE NIGHT OF THE SHIRTS


Oh pile of white shirts who is coming
to breathe in your shapes to carry your numbers
to appear
what hearts
are moving toward their garments here
their days
what troubles beating between arms

you look upward through
each other saying nothing has happened
and it has gone away and is sleeping
having told the same story
and we exist from within
eyes of the gods

you lie on your backs
and the wounds are not made
the blood has not heard
the boat has not turned to stone
and the dark wires to the bulb
are full of the voice of the unborn


SHOE REPAIRS

*for Charles Hanzlicek*

Long after the scheduled deaths of animals
their skins made up into couples
have arrived here
empty
from many turnings
between the ways of men
and men

In a side street
by brown walls over a small light
the infinite routes
which they follow a little way
come together
to wait in rows in twos
soles
eyes of masks
from a culture lost forever

We will know the smell
in another life
stepping down
barefoot into this Ark
seeing it lit up but empty
the destined racks
done with the saved pairs
that went out to die each alone


AGE


These fields of thistles are the old
who believed in the day they had
and held it like an army
now that they are blind
with an alien whiteness clutching their feet
their hair blows into the sea
———

Ancient sockets
as the snow fell you looked up
full of milk
saying there was something we did not find
it was a child
how could we recognize it since it was never born
———

As they enter extinction the birds join the vast
flocks of prayers circling over the gulf
in the unreturning light
and the old think it is snow
falling slowly and stopping in the day sky
or the stars the stars

## LAUGHTER

The great gods are blind or pretend to be

finding that I am among men I open my eyes
and they shake

## SNOWFALL

*For my mother*

Some time in the dark hours
it seemed I was a spark climbing
the black road
with my death helping me up
a white self helping me up
like a brother
growing
but this morning
I see that the silent kin I loved as a child
have arrived all together in the night
from the old country
they remembered
and everything remembers
I eat from the hands
of what for years have been junipers
the taste has not changed
I am beginning
again
but a bell rings in some village I do not know
and cannot hear
and in the sunlight snow drops from branches
leaving its name in the air
and a single footprint

brother

# BANISHMENT IN WINTER

*for Richard Howard*

From the north the wands the long
questions of light
descend among us from my country
even by day
and their discoveries are recorded
beyond the silence
blue eyes watch needles
oh little by little it will be seen who remembers
the cold dusk crossing the pastures
the black hay ridged
along the darkness
the color of snow
at night
So even by day
the wands reach toward the outer river
toward the deep shadows
inquiring and above us
like stars in a slow negative
the migrants
the true migrants
already immeasurably far
the dark migrants
the souls
move outward into the cold
but will it ever be
dark again in my country
where hanging from lamp posts
the good
fill the streets with their steady light

# FOOTPRINTS ON THE GLACIER

Where the wind
year round out of the gap
polishes everything
here this day are footprints like my own
the first ever
frozen
pointing up into the cold

and last night someone
marched and marched on the candle flame
hurrying
a painful road
and I heard the echo a long time afterwards
gone and some connection of mine

I scan the high slopes for a dark speck
that was lately here
I pass my hands
over the melted wax
like a blind man
they are all
moving into their seasons at last
my bones face each other trying
to remember a question

nothing moves while I watch
but here the black trees
are the cemetery of a great battle
and behind me as I turn
I hear names leaving the bark
in growing numbers and flying north

## TALE

After many winters the moss
finds the sawdust crushed bark chips
and says old friend
old friend

## FULL MOONLIGHT IN SPRING

Night sends this white eye
to her brother the king of the snow

## NIGHT WIND

All through the dark the wind looks
for the grief it belongs to
but there was no place
for that any more

I have looked too
and seen only the nameless hunger
watching us out of the stars
ancestor

and the black fields

## MIDNIGHT IN EARLY SPRING

At one moment a few old leaves come in
frightened
and lie down together and stop moving
the nights now go in threes
as in a time of danger
the flies
sleep like sentries on the darkened panes

some alien blessing
is on its way to us
some prayer ignored for centuries
is about to be granted to the prayerless
in this place

who were you
cold voice born in captivity
rising
last martyr of a hope
last word of a language
last son
other half of grief
who were you

so that we may know why
when the streams
wake tomorrow and we are free

# AS THOUGH I WAS WAITING FOR THAT

Some day it will rain
from a cold place
and the sticks and stones will darken their faces
the salt will wash from the worn gods
of the good
and mourners will be waiting
on the far sides of the hills

and I will remember the calling
recognized at the wrong hours
long since
and hands a long way back
that will have forgotten
and a direction will have abandoned my feet
their way
that offered
itself vainly day after day
at last gone
like a color or the cloth at elbows

I will stir when it is getting dark
and stand when it is too late
as though I was waiting for that
and start out into the weather
into emptiness
passing the backs of trees
of the rain of the mourners
the backs of names the back
of darkness

for no reason
hearing no voice
with no promise
praying to myself
be clear

# THE PLUMBING

*for Adrienne Rich*

New silence
between the end and the beginning
The planet that was never named
because it was dark
climbs into the evening
nothing else moves
moon stars the black laundry the hour
have stopped and are looking away
the lungs stand
a frozen forest
into which no air comes

they go on standing like shadows
of the plumbing
that is all that is left
of the great city
the buildings vanished the windows
extinct the smoke with its strings of names
wiped away
and its fire
at the still note
the throwing of a switch

only these pipes
bereft of stairs of elevators
of walls of girders
awakened from lamps from roofs
grow into the night
crowding upward in rows
to desolate heights their blind hope
and their black mouths locked open hollow stars
between the dark planets
a famine a worship the heirs
of the dials

among their feet
my heart is still beating by itself
thinking it understands and might feed them


## BEGINNING OF THE PLAINS

On city bridges steep as hills I change countries
and this according to the promise
is the way home

where the cold has come from
with its secret baggage

in the white sky the light flickering
like the flight of a wing

nothing to be bought in the last
dim shops
before the plain begins
few shelves kept only by children
and relatives there for the holiday
who know nothing

wind without flags
marching into the city
to the rear

I recognize the first hunger
as the plains start
under my feet

ASCENT

I have climbed a long way
there are my shoes
minute larvae
the dark parents
I know they will wait there looking up
until someone leads them away

by the time they have got to the place
that will do for their age
and are in there with nothing to say
the shades drawn
nothing but wear
between them

I may have reached the first
of the bare meadows
recognized in the air
the eyes by their blankness
turned
knowing myself seen by the lost
silent
barefoot choir

THE HULK

The water itself is leaving the harbor
a gleam waiting in lines
to be gone
and there I am
the small child the small child
alone with the huge ship at last

It must be named for silence
the iron whale asleep on its side
in the breathless port
a name rusted out
in an unknown
unknown language

And no one will come
to call me by any name
the ropes end like water
the walls lie on their backs
bodies dusted with light
I can sail if we sail
I can wander
through the rusting passages forever
with my fear by the hand
by the hand
and no father

## FEAR

Fear
there is
fear in fear the name the blue and green walls
falling of and numbers fear the veins that
when they were opened fear flowed from and
these forms it took a ring a ring a ring
a bit of grass green swan's down gliding on
fear into fear and the hatred and something
in everything and it is my death's
disciple leg and fear no he would not
have back those lives again and their fear as
he feared he would say but he feared more he
did not fear more he did fear more
in everything it is there a long time

as I was and it is within those
blue and green walls that the actual
verification has and in fact will
take the form of a ring a ring a ring
took I should say the figure in the hall
of the glass giants the third exhibition
on the right is fear I am I fear and
the rain falling fear red fear yellow fear
blue and green for their depth etcetera
fear etcetera water fire earth air
etcetera in everything made of
human agency or divine fear is
in the answer also and shall pierce thy
bosom too fear three gathered together
four five etcetera the brightest day
the longest day its own fear the light
itself the nine village tailors fear
their thread if not their needles if not
their needles in everything and it is
here this is New York and aside from that
fear which under another name in
every stone Abraham is buried it
is fear the infant's lovely face the
grass green alleys oh at about the third
hour of the night it being in those parts
still light there came fear my loving fear
in everything it is next the baker the
candlestick maker if you know what I
answer at that point and fear the little
cobbler his last is one fear and there is
fear in all shoes in the shoe line the clothes
line any clothes the blood line any in
everything it is the third button
the book books fear the bottle and what it
contains everything a life death the spirit
staring inward on nothing there and
the sunken vessel the path through the shadow
the shadow of me me or if I am not

suddenly fear coming from the west
singing the great song there was no need
fear no crying and others would sift
the salt in silence in fear the house
where I am familiar in all your
former lives remembered your parents
fear and fear theirs of your parents by
your parents and for your parents shall not
perish from this deciding everything
and it is deciding strike out Mr
Mrs Miss I am alone little stones
fear forgetting forgets remembering
it is my loving fear the mouth of my
seeing fear I am awake I am not
awake and fear no bones like my own
brother fear my death's sister and high on
the cliff face the small arched door from which
a man could fear or be in the winking
of an eye the tapping of the second
finger of the left hand the wind itself
fear I am alone forever I am
fear I am alone I fear I am
not alone couldn't tell your breath from fear
for it is your breath I do it and I'm
supposed to explain it too I fear I
completed my fear in everything there is
fear and I would speak for myself but fear
says logic follows but I advance in
everything and so discovery
geography history law comedy
fear law poetry major prophets
minor prophets that pass in the night
it is a mother and a guiding light
moving across fear before which they burn
in rows in red glass bleeding upwards their
hearts smoke in the gusts on earth as it is
in heaven with the sentence beginning

before the heavens were or the earth
had out of fear been called and any began
to be fear the bird feather by feather
note by note eye by eye pierced he is my
neighbor in the uttermost parts of aye
and shall I couple heaven when the fear
shall fear and those who walked in fear shall see
fear their very form and being for
their eyes shall be opened it was going
on in everything and I forgot but if you
stand here you can see fear the new building
starting to rise from which our children
will fear the stilted dogs the insects
who do not exist the dead burning
as candles oh dark flames cold lights in
everything without you the ship coming
in and a long way that I would never
traverse before fear had followed that
scent faster than a mortal bearing fear
I'm telling you I'm asking you I'm dying
I'm here today this is New York I'm more
than any one person or two persons
can stand fear the way down in everything
the way up is the same fear the next place
the next I said fear come on you it's you
I'm addressing get into line you're going
never fear there is a hair hanging by
everything it is the edges of things
the light of things do you see nothing
in them burning and the long crying
didn't you hear that either I mean
you again fear it's a strange name not
for a stranger ma'am he said lying I
mean there is you fear me fear but you
must not imagine fear through which the present
moves like a star that I or that
you either clearly and from the beginning

could ever again because from the beginning
there is fear in everything and it is
me and always was in everything it
is me


PILATE


It has
a life of its own however long it
served Pharaoh and so a heaven of its
own to which its own blood calls which should be
heard with respect when they call crucify
crucify him of its own why should you
not see it unless it is walking arm
in arm with objects which you think you can see
without it when lo empire itself
is not visible

and a future of its own
the prophecies waking without names in
strange lands on unborn tongues those syllables
resurrected staring is that heaven
all the pain to find its hands again old
but you must not suppose that because of
the centurions' reports eclipses
on frontiers and the beards there blowing
through wooden fences dead men but there no
flies in that wind crying sand only
the long arrows and the kissing arrows
through which his wife coming with her spillage
of dreams because of this man but it is
the broken windows that look to the future
and empire is the viewing as different
so a dream itself and how can a man voyage
on more than one bark one trireme one skiff

with one oar at one time even after
the washing is heard on that shore and
the one oar

and you should not imagine either
that you yourselves are later or far or
otherwise else above all those tongues tongues
lit at the tops of arms under
the lungless banners the dread in amber
the silence rolling on before the shadows
burning on the walls with dark cries or going
home a long way through the baths
the gowns dripping the feet growing barer
and the dark flights vanishing into the
cracks in the day

it is termed an alien
judgment they are like that and can force then
be held accountable that has no life
of its own the dark wine dark throats the call
the call that hangs in the banners until
it falls as shall the banners fall
from the walls the walls from the sky its smoke
its eagles what was I put here to change
I was not put here to change

could I change myself my hands
and their dreams a life of their own with its
own heaven own future own windows
washing can I change what they do before
I am born for they will do it without me
arm in arm with objects but lo myself
is not visible to these this man the life
of its own without me its smoke its eagles
and wooden fences and tonight the hands
in the outer circles of the soldiers'
corner fires later than the last meal
gesturing in the reeling night washing

in darkness afterwards will go home
and the darkness will let itself down
into their prayers


SHORE


We turned hearing the same note
of the flute far inland unfaltering and
unknown to each other but already
wrapped in the silence that we would each wear
we left two the hills one the valley before
day entered the pearl and we drew
together as streams descend through their
darkness to the shore

there it was even then by that horn light
of an old skin to be seen approaching
out of the black the lifted prow which waves
touched and fled from on the engraved flood
the scar on the wooden breast climbing above
the breast and the after vessel gazing
up and back at the night the family
the resemblance invisible to us
as it bore in bore in rapidly
to the rocky plain the eggs of venerable
stones the leaden shingle washed and washed under
the shrieks of curlews and that unbreaking
note as of a planet

making in fast toward our eyes fixed
on the uncolored bow one massed and older
jutting in velvet hat and the gown dark
to the shingle beyond whom the sky
whitened out of the gnarled littoral
the other no nearer the waves still young

a fisherman bareheaded in boots
it is my feet that are bare and others
may have gathered behind us the fires
would have been lit at home but we no longer
see behind us

and we hear nothing above the haul
of tongues leaving the shore to the flute's
accompaniment silent flocks pass
on their black journeys it is making in
at a speed that ignores the steely elements
we are waiting waiting what it was carrying
in the early hours as we believed
it could no longer have borne living when the white
shadow gained on heaven and a figure
like the beam of a lantern seemed
to stand in the bark but now though the hollow
board is plainly nearer the light will set
soon where it first rose and we get by heart
the spot where the shingle will scrape in the night
if the keel touches


PSALM: OUR FATHERS


I am the son of joy but does he know me
I am the son of hope but he ascends into heaven
I am the son of peace but I was put out to nurse
I am the son of grief after the brother was lost but I have opened an eye
    in the life where it was he who lived
I am the son of a shadow and I draw my blinds out of respect but I cleave
    uneasily to the light
I am the son of love but where is my home and where the black baptis-
    mal cup and the frightened eyes that would still come to the names
    I gave them
I am the son of the tribe of Apher which set up empty tents and camped

where it could defend them and was remembered for them but I
have discovered that the unknowable needs no defense
I am the son of the temptations of the rocks but there have been some
between
I am the son of fear but I find out for myself
I am the son of the first fish who climbed ashore but the news has not yet
reached my bowels
I am the son of three flowers the pink the rose and the other or its effigy
in skin for neither of which was I taught a name and I shudder at
their withering all three but they will survive me
I am the son of the future but she shows me only her mourning veil
I am the son of the future but my own father
I am the son of the future but where is my home and the black baptismal
cup and the warning voice from the bushes under the kitchen
window saying that they were not my parents
I am the son of a glass tombstone in a fresh plowed field whose furrows
sit in rows studying the inscriptions of dew the sole name life tears
as the sun rises but there are no more voices on that river
I am the son of the water-thief who got away and founded a bare-faced
dynasty but the fountains are still following
I am the son of a plaster bone in the oldest reconstruction in Millenial
Hall but all my ages are one
I am the son of the cymbal of Bethel that answered like a cracked bowl
to the instruments of ivory of bone iron wood brass hair gold gut
glass through all the generations of the sacred orchestra a maimed
voice before the throne with waiting as it was for its like to be
found its twin its other face sun socket identical disc the very metal
the other half its cymbal so that it could sound its own true note
but only one had been made
I am the son of an unsuspected wealth but I may labor all my life and
leave nothing but a grain of mustard seed
I am the son of thanksgiving but its language is strange in my mouth
I am the son of the glove of an upper river and the glove of a tree but
there were four rivers all told around the garden and I tasted of salt
from the beginning
I am the son of the fourth son in the right hand jars on the second row of
the seventh shelf above the glass footwalk on the fifth floor in the
ninth bay of the eighty-third room of the T18 wing of the heart

division of the St. Luke's Memorial Index but he died in a strange
land before I was born

I am the son of Cargarran who was an ant in the time of the noseless
emperors and was accorded great emulation an urn of amber and a
flag to fly his picture on for he fought with the plague of crane
seeds until darkness came to his rescue but I have use to be
frightened if I wake if I remember if a tax is mentioned or it is
Thursday

I am the son of seven promises the last of them to live to see it again but
the womb may not have been listening

I am the son of the word Still after the angels came to the door in her
barren age but on that same day she lost her memory and she gave
birth without understanding

I am the son of a drunken rape at a veterans' convention in a brutal
empire bandaged with the arguments of empires but hallowed by
thy name

I am the son of the starvation of the Utes the tortures and gassing of
the Jews the interrogation of suspects the burning of villages the
throat of the antelope the amputations of the domesticated the cries
of the extinct and I plead ignorance ignorance but it would be no
better to be an orphan

I am the son of the ark that was carried empty before the tribes in the
wilderness but I walk because the times have changed and there is
no one behind

I am the son of the statue of Hamalid the Great The Weight of God that
was re-named Vengeance in a different tongue and that with raised
knife still shouts its incomprehensible syllable to the dark square
with one foot on the illegible date of death and no apparent sex any
longer but it was modeled on a jailer's dead wife

I am the son of four elements fire darkness salt and vertigo but I dance as
though they were strangers

I am the son of the cloud Cynian that appeared as a torn white breast
above Herod and was not recognized but I acknowledge its vatic
suffering still visible in the bruised haze of the ridges

I am of the blood of the ash shrew whose remains have not been found
but whose characteristics have been deduced from my teeth my
mistakes the atrophied ear at the heart of each of my fingerprints
and the size of the door at the base of the skull where now the

performers enter each with his eye fixed on the waiting instrument
I am the son of the bird fire that has no eyes but sings to itself after
    waiting alone and silent in the alien wood
I am the son of fear but it means I am never lost
I am the son of terrible labors but triumph comes to the flags that have
    done nothing
I am the son of pain but time nurses me
I am the son of nobody but when I go the islands turn black
I am the son of the first Sabbath but after me cometh the eighth day
I am the son of hunger hunger and hunger in an unbroken line back to
    the mouths of the coelenterates but even I have been filled
I am the son of remorse in a vein of fossils but I might not have been
I am the son of division but the nails the wires the hasps the bolts the
    locks the traps the wrapping that hold me together are part of the
    inheritance
I am the son of indifference but neglect is a stage in the life of the gods
I am the son of No but memory bathes its knowledge in desire
I am the son of blindness but I watch the light stretch one wing
I am the son of a silence in heaven but I cried and the dark angels went
    on falling
I am the son of things as they are but I know them for the most part only
    as they are remembered
I am the son of farewells and one of me will not come back but one of
    me never forgets
I am the son of violence the ignorance herald but the seal is royal
I am the son of stars never seen never to be seen for we will be gone
    before their light reaches us but the decisions they demand are with
    us
    now now
I am the son of love but I lose you in the palm of my hand
I am the son of prisoners but I was got out in the form of a gold tooth a
    picture of two elders in a platinum locket a pair of eyeglasses with
    rims of white metal one pearl earring a knife with a picture of
    Jerusalem on the silver handle and I am being reassembled and
    keep finding myself and beginning again the process of reunion
I am the son of hazard but does my prayer reach you o star of the
    uncertain
I am the son of blindness but nothing that we have made watches us

I am the son of untruth but I have seen the children in Paradise walking
    in pairs each hand in hand with himself
I am the son of the warder but he was buried with his keys
I am the son of the light but does it call me Samuel or Jonah
I am the son of a wish older than water but I needed till now
I am the son of ghosts clutching the world like roads but tomorrow I
    will go a new way
I am the son of ruins already among us but at moments I have found
    hope beyond doubt beyond desert beyond reason and such that I
    have prayed O wounds come back from death and be healed
I am the son of hazard but go on with the story you think is yours
I am the son of love but the hangmen are my brothers
I am the son of love but the islands are black
I am the son of love for which parent the blood gropes in dread as
    though it were naked and for which cause the sun hangs in a cage
    of light
    and we are his pains


## CUCKOO MYTH


Stay with the cuckoo I heard
then the cuckoo I heard
then I was born

cuckoo cuckoo she
that from hiding
sings
from dark coverts
from gates where ghosts
stand open
cuckoo
from loss the light rises
a voice that bears with it its hiding

cuckoo that in her time

sings unseen
because the wing beheld
by the unhappy
shall fall
flew again to the first season
to the undivided
returned from there bringing
to the creatures Love
a light for the unhappy
but the light bore with it
its hiding

cuckoo that sings
in echoes
because the voice that the falling follow
falls
flew again under the years
to the unturning
returned from there bringing
to the world Death
a light for the unhappy
but a light rising
from loss

cuckoo cuckoo
that through time sings changing
now she has gone again


SECOND PSALM: THE SIGNALS


When the ox-horn sounds in the buried hills
  of Iceland
  I am alone
  my shadow runs back into me to hide
  and there is not room for both of us

and the dread
when the ox-horn sounds on the blue stairs
    where the echoes are my mother's name
    I am alone
    as milk spilled in a street
    white instrument
    white hand
    white music
when the ox-horn is raised like a feather in one
    of several rivers
    not all of which I have come to
    and the note starts toward the sea
    I am alone
    as the optic nerve of the blind
    though in front of me it is written
    *This is the end of the past*
    *Be happy*
when the ox-horn sounds from its tassels of blood
    I always seem to be opening
    a book an envelope the top of a well
    none of them mine
    a tray of gloves has been set down
    beside my hands
    I am alone
    as the hour of the stopped clock
when the ox-horn is struck by its brother
    and the low grieving denial
    gropes forth again with its black hands
    I am alone
    as one stone left to pray in the desert
    after god had unmade himself
    I am
    I still am
when the ox-horn sounds over the dead oxen
    the guns grow light in hands
    I the fearer
    try to destroy me the fearing
    I am alone

as a bow that has lost its nerve
my death sinks into me to hide
as water into stones
before a great cold
when the ox-horn is raised in silence
someone's breath is moving over my face
like the flight of a fly
but I am in this world
without you
I am alone as the sadness surrounding
what has long ministered to our convenience
alone as the note of the horn
as the human voice
saddest of instruments
as a white grain of sand falling in a still sea
alone as the figure she unwove each night alone

alone
as I will be


THE PENS


In the city of fire the eyes
look upward
there is no memory
except the smoke writing writing *wait*
*wai*
*w*
under the light that has
the stars inside it
the white
invisible stars they also
writing

and unable to read

# THE FORBEARS

I think I was cold in the womb
shivering I
remember
cold too I think did my brother suffer
who slept before me there
and cold I am sure was John in the early
as in the earlier
dawn all they
even whose names are anonymous
now known for their cold only
I believe they quaking lay
beforetime there
dancing like teeth and I
was them all foretelling me
if not the name the trembling
if not the time the dancing
if not the hour the longing
in the round night


# VOICE

*for Jane Kirstein 1916–1968*

By now you will have met
no one
my elder sister
you will have sat
by her breath in the dark
she will have told you I don't know what
in the way she remembers whatever it is
that's how she is
I never see her
but it's you I miss

by now she'll have sat around you
in a circle holding your hand
saying she's listening but
you'll hear you'll hear what she says
to everyone but especially to my friends
is it good what she tells you
is it anything I'd know

her own brother
but I still remember only
afterwards
and we're all like this

by now
more and more I remember
what isn't so
your voice
as I heard it in a dream
the night you died
when it was no longer yours


LAST PEOPLE


Our flowers are numbered
we no longer know where
phrases
last messages written on the white petals
appear as they wither
but in whose language
how could we ask

other messages emerge in the smells
we listen
listen
as they grow fainter

when we go home
with what we have got
when we climb the stairs reciting ancient deeds
the seas grow deeper
that we rose from
when we open the door
when we shut the door
the dust
goes on falling in our heads
goes on falling in our hearts

at the day's end
all our footsteps are added up
to see how near

what will be left
how long will the old men's kingdom survive
the lines of pebbles signifying
house
tea cups on stones
who will feed the dogs
it was like this before

it was like this before
triumphs long in the preparing
stumbled through cracking
film light
and we seem to have known
their faces crumpling just before
they vanished
like papers burning
while the features of plants rose out of plants
to watch them pass
to remember

# THIRD PSALM: THE SEPTEMBER VISION

*for Galway Kinnell*

I see the hand in which the sun rises
 a memory looking
 for a mind
I see black days black days
 the minds of stones
 going
 but likewise coming
 their sealed way
I see an empty bird cage
 a memory looking
 for a heart
 asked to feel more
 feels less
I see an empty bird flying
 and its song follows me
 with my own name
 with the sound of the ice
 of my own name
 breaking
I see the eyes of that bird
 in each light
 in rain
 in mirrors
 in eyes
 in spoons
I see clear lakes float over us
 touching us with their hems
 and they carry away secrets
 they never brought
I see tongues being divided
 and the birth of speech
 that must grow
 in pain
 and set out for Nineveh

I see a moth approaching
        like one ear of an invisible animal
        and I am not calling
I see bells riding dead horses
        and there was never a silence like this

        oh objects come and talk with us while you can


AFTER THE HARVESTS


Every night hears the sound of rain
it is the roofer's widow looking for him
in her glass sleep


NOW IT IS CLEAR


Now it is clear to me that no leaves are mine
no roots are mine
that wherever I go I will be a spine of smoke in the forest
and the forest will know it
we will both know it

and that the birds vanish because of something
that I remember
flying from me as though I were a great wind
as the stones settle into the ground
the trees into themselves
staring as though I were a great wind
which is what I pray for

it is clear to me that I cannot return
but that some of us will meet once more
even here
like our own statues
and some of us still later without names
and some of us will burn with the speed
of endless departures

and be found and lost no more


## MAN WITH ONE LEAF IN OCTOBER NIGHT


The leaves turn black when they have learned how to fly
so does the day
but in the wind of the first hours of darkness
sudden joy sent
from an unknown tree
I have not deserved you


## WOMAN FROM THE RIVER


I thought it was an empty doorway
standing there by me
and it was you
I can see that you stood that way
cold as a pillar
while they made the stories about you

## LATE NIGHT IN AUTUMN

In the hills ahead a pain is moving its light
through the dark skies of a self
it is on foot I think
it is old
the year will soon be home and its own hear it
but in some house of my soul
a calling is coming in again off the cold mountains
and here one glove is hanging from each window
oh long way to go


## STILL AFTERNOON LIGHT

Known love standing in deep grove
new love naked on plain

dance record
from before I was born

played with a new needle

no dancing


## KIN

Up the west slope before dark
shadow of my smoke
old man

climbing the old men's mountain

at the end
birds lead something down to me
it is silence

they leave it with me
in the dark
it is from them

that I am descended

## MEMORY OF SPRING

The first composer
could hear only what he could write

## SIGNS

Half my life ago
watching the river birds

———

Dawn
white bird let go

———

Strange
to be any place

———

Leaves understand flowers
well enough

———

Each sleeper
troubled

by his light

———

Waves sever
sever

———

Silence
is my shepherd

———

Born once
born forever

———

Small dog barking
far down in walls

———

The wind wakes in the dark
knowing it's happened

———

Music stops
on the far side of a bay

———

Don't walk

———

Window
in the house
of a blind man

———

A shout
darkening the roofs

———

Quick smile
like a shoe's

———

No keys to the shadows
the wind shakes them

———

Silent rivers
fall toward us
without explaining

———

City
stands by a river
with torches

———

Not part of the country
part of the horizon

———

Blind
remembering me as a child

———

Bitterness of seeds
a form of knowledge

———

Men
until they enter that building

———

Look at their shoes
to see how gravely
they are hurt

———

Deaf
listens for his heart

hears name of a great star
never seen

———

Snow
falls in plum orchards
as though it had been there before

———

Bell spills
sky darkens

———

Appear
not as they are
but as what prevents them

———

Walk
———

Clear night
fish
jumping at stars


## THE PAW


I return to my limbs with the first
gray light
and here is the gray paw under my hand
the she-wolf Perdita
has come back
to sleep beside me
her spine pressed knuckle to knuckle
down my front
her ears lying against my ribs
on the left side where the heart beats

and she takes its sound for the pulsing
of her paws
we are coursing the black sierra once more
in the starlight
oh Perdita

we are racing over the dark auroras
you and I with no shadow
with no shadow
in the same place

so she came back
again in the black hours
running before the open sack
we have run
these hours together

again
there is blood
on the paw under my fingers
flowing
there is blood then
on the black heights again
in her tracks
our tracks
but vanishing like a shadow

and there is blood
against my ribs again
oh Perdita
she is more beautiful after every wound
as though they were stars
I know
how the haunches are hollowed
stretched out in the dark
at full speed like a constellation
I hear
her breath moving on the fields of frost
my measure
I beat faster
her blood wells through my fingers
my eyes shut to see her
again
my way

before the stars fall
and the mountains go out
and the void wakes
and it is day

but we are gone

# THE THREAD

Unrolling the black thread
through the tunnel
you come to the wide wall
of shoes
the soles standing
out in the air you breathe
crowded from side to side
floor to ceiling
and no names
and no door
and the bodies
stacked before them like bottles
generation upon
generation
upon generation
with their threads
asleep in their hands
and the tunnel is full
of their bodies
from there
all the way to the end of the mountain
the beginning of time
the light of day
the bird
and you are unrolling
the Sibyll's song
that is trying to reach her
beyond your dead

# THE BLESSING

There is a blessing on the wide road
the eggshell road the baked highway
there is a blessing an old woman
walking fast following him

pace of a child following him

he left today
in a fast car

until or unless
she is with him
the traffic flows through her
as though she were air
or not there

she can speak only to him
she can tell him
what only he can hear

she can save him
once

it might be enough

she is hurrying

he is making good time
his breath comes more easily
he is still troubled at moments
by the feeling
that he has forgotten something
but he thinks he is escaping a terrible
horseman

BEGINNING

Long before spring
king of the black cranes
rises one day
from the black
needle's eye
on the white plain
under the white sky

the crown turns
and the eye
drilled clear through his head
turns
it is north everywhere
come out he says

come out then
the light is not yet
divided
it is a long way
to the first
anything
come even so
we will start
bring your nights with you


THE FIRST DARKNESS

Maybe he does not even have to exist
to exist in departures
then the first darkness falls
even there a shining is flowing from all the stones

though the eyes are not yet made that can see it
saying Blessèd
are ye



THE CHAFF


Those who cannot love the heavens or the earth
beaten from the heavens and the earth
eat each other
those who cannot love each other
beaten from each other
eat themselves
those who cannot love themselves
beaten from themselves
eat a terrible bread
kneaded in the morning shrouded all day
baked in the dark
whose sweet smell brings the chaff flying like empty hands
through the turning sky night after night
calling with voices of young birds
to its wheat



FOURTH PSALM: THE CEREMENTS


She made him a roof with her hands
    from his own voice she wove
    the walls to stop the wind
    with his own dreams she painted the windows
    each with its kingdom
    and the doors were mirrors she fashioned
    of his eyes

but when she opened it he was gone

gone the vision
gone
the witness

She made him a cage of wishes
    he helped when he could
    helped long
    and indeed with all the heavy parts

    but when she opened it

She made him a net of consents
    where he might turn in his own place
    like an eye in its veins
    a globe in its hours
    she hung it with tears
    with both of theirs

    but when she opened it he was gone

    gone
    the asking

She made him a box of some sweet wood
    she knew he remembered from his childhood
    in corners rose columns she had painted like smoke
    she drew a star inside the lid

    but when she opened it

She made him a bed such as the fates have
    in the palms of the newly born
    but there they do not lay them down
    they have risen

and when she opened it
he was gone

gone the cry the laughter

They made him a fence of names
each with its story
like his own teeth
they laid claim
to his ears
but he had others

when they opened the echoes even the echoes
he had gone

They made him an ark of the one tree
and places for him builded in
two of every kind

but before the rain came
he was gone

laws of the hands gone
night of the veins gone
gone the beating in the temples

and every face in the sky

THE WEB

So it's mind
this leg of a thin gray traveling animal
caught in the web again
tearing
in the stocking of blood

the old scars waking opening
in the form of a web

the seamless fabric itself bleeding
where it clings

and all this time dark wings
cries
cries flying over at a great height

o web

over the sand you are woven
over the water you are woven
over the snow you are woven
over the grass you are woven
over the mountains you are woven
over the heads of the lambs you are woven
over the fish you are woven
over the faces you are woven
over the clouds you are woven
over the pain itself you are woven

the tears glint on you like a dew
the blood is spreading wherever you have held me
the days and the nights
keep their distance
without a sound

but I remember also the ringing spaces
when I have crossed you like a hand on a harp
and even now
in the echoless sky the birds pursue our music

hoping to hear it again

# LETTER

By the time you read this

    it is dark on the next page

    the mourners sleep there
    feeling their feet in the tide

    before me in the dusk an animal rose and vanished
    your name

    you have been with me also in the descent
    the winter
    you remember
    how many things come to one name
    hoping to be fed

    it changes but the name for it
    is still the same
    I tell you it is still the same

    hungry birds in the junipers
    all night
    snow

    all night

    by the time you read this

    the address of the last house
    that we will sleep in together on earth
    will have been paid as a price
    dialed on a telephone
    worn as identification

passed on speedometers in unmarked places
multiplied by machines
divided divided
undistracted
standing guard over us all the time
over past future
present
faceless angel

whom each rain washes nearer to himself

but I tell you
by the time you read this
wherever

I tell you


INSCRIPTION FACING WESTERN SEA


Lord of each wave comes in
campaign finished ten thousand miles
years clashes winds dead moons
riderless horses no messages
he lays down flag bowing quickly and retires
his flag
sun waits to take him home
flag fades
sand
stars gather again to watch the war

## THE SADNESS

Thinking of you I lean over silent water
this head
appears
the earth turns
the sky has no motion
one by one my eyelashes free themselves
and fall
and meet themselves for the first time
the last time


## THE CALLING UNDER THE BREATH

Through the evening
the mountains approach over the desert
sails from a windless kingdom

silence runs through the birds
their shadows freeze

where are you

where are you where are you
I have set sail on a fast mountain
whose shadow is everywhere

## SUNSET AFTER RAIN

Old cloud passes mourning her daughter
can't hear what anyone tells her
every minute is one of the doors that never opened

———

Little cold stream wherever I go
you touch the heart
night follows

———

The darkness is cold
because the stars do not believe in each other

## ELEGY

Who would I show it to

## IN THE TIME OF THE BLOSSOMS

Ash tree
sacred to her who sails in
from the one sea
all over you leaf skeletons
fine as sparrow bones
stream out motionless
on white heaven
staves of one
unbreathed music
Sing to me

# WRITINGS
## TO AN
## UNFINISHED
## ACCOMPANIMENT
### (1973)

EARLY ONE SUMMER

Years from now
someone will come upon a layer of birds
and not know what he is listening for

these are days
when the beetles hurry through dry grass
hiding pieces of light they have stolen


EYES OF SUMMER

All the stones have been us
and will be again
as the sun touches them you can feel
sun
and remember waking with no face
knowing that it was summer
still
when the witnesses
day after day are blinded
so that they will forget nothing


END OF SUMMER

High above us a chain of white buckets
full of old light going home

now even the things that we do
reach us after long journeys
and we have changed

## THE DISTANCES

When you think of the distances
you recall
that we are immortal

you think of them setting out from us
all of them setting out
from us
and none dies and none is forgotten

and all over the world there are dams
lying on their backs
thinking of the sea


## LOOKING BACK

Oh we have moved forward in pain

what has broken off every rock

have they each suffered
each time
wanting to stay
have they not

Before the first cell
the sands

## SONG OF MAN CHIPPING AN ARROWHEAD

Little children you will all go
but the one you are hiding
will fly


## THE SILENCE BEFORE HARVEST

The harps the harps
standing in fields
standing

and dark hands
playing

somewhere else the sound
sound
will arrive
light from a star

## CAT GHOSTS

### I

Years after
in a kitchen of another country
you're still hungry

### II

In the heat of the day
your shadow comes back
to lie on your stone


## LETTER TO THE HEART

Again the cry that it's late
and the islands
are just beginning to rise


## MEMORY OF THE LOSS OF WINGS

An hour comes
to close a door behind me
the whole of night opens before me

## THE OLD BOAST

Listen natives of a dry place
from the harpist's fingers
rain

## THE DAY

If you could take the day by the hand
even now and say Come Father
calling it by your own name
it might rise in its blindness with all
its knuckles and curtains
and open the eyes it was born with

## THE CLEAR SKIES

The clouds that touch us out of clear skies

they are eyes that we lost
long ago on the mountain
and lose
every day on the dark mountain
under clear skies

and because we lose them we say they are old
because they are blind we say
that they cannot find us
that their cloudy gaze
cannot touch us
on our mountain

because we have lost whoever
they are calling
we say that they are not calling
us


## TO BE SUNG WHILE STILL LOOKING

Have you seen my memory
in better light
no sound for the moment
as there might
with those faces
and the gates about to close
that never do

Have you seen my memory
that hardly knew
what to do with the flags
at an age where nothing dies
but the windows are open
and same eyes
as it rolls with no echo
on the thankless roads

Have you seen my memory
after years
by fallen schools
with the smell of coats on it
and smaller coats
when there is time enough
have you seen the promises
or the tracks have you noticed
the age of the air
once it's clear

Have you seen my memory
minus the fancy words
have you looked in the cases
where I kept my mind
to tell me things
such as she lay in shallow water
in shallow water she lies
and she comes out to me
the first day
not far from home

Have you seen
my memory
the flame far from the candles


UNDER THE MIGRANTS


Winter is almost upon us
and in the south there is a battle

every day silent thunder from there
light going up like a shout

each of us is alone
when we close our eyes
the roads are strips of death

when we open our eyes the bandages
go on unwinding
back into the north the whiteness

on the avenues trucks rumble southward
to be seen no more

can you hear yourself we cannot

flocks of single hands are all flying
southward

from us

and the clocks all night all day
point that way


## ON THE SILENT ANNIVERSARY OF A REUNION

Each of these hours has been to you first
and stared
and forgotten
but I know the burnt smell
in their clothes their clothes
and know that you have at last unwoven the charred wick
into a cold black fan
and are sitting by its light
with your hands turning to stone


## ON EACH JOURNEY

As on each journey there is
a silence that goes with it
to its end let us go
with each other
though the sun with its choirs of distance
rises between us though it
were to hang there the past like a day
that would burn unmoved forever

and only we went on
each alone each with nothing
but a silence


BEYOND YOU


Even when the dry wells of black honey
overflow into the winter starlight
and their stars know them at last
and taste and are young
when the shrivelled boats that have carried the sun
wake one by one face down by the river
and rise blind to sing where they are
if I can stand I will be standing by the last one
calling you
who are so near that I cannot believe you
and when I call the calling begins
beyond you


THEIR WEEK


The loneliness of Sundays grows
tall there as the light
and from it they weave
bells of different sizes
to hang in empty cupboards and in doorways
and from branches
like blossoms like fruit
and in barns
and in each room like lamps
like the light

they believe it was on a Sunday
that the animals were divided
so that the flood could happen
and on a Sunday that we were severed
from the animals
with a wound that never heals
but is still the gate where the nameless
cries out

they believe that everything
that is divided
was divided on a Sunday
and they weave the bells
whose echoes
are all the days in the week


OLD FLAG


When I want to tell of the laughing throne
and of how all the straw in the world
records the sounds of dancing
the man called Old Flag is there
in the doorway
and my words might be his dogs

when I want to speak of the sweet light
on a grassy shore
he is there
and my words have never forgotten the bitter
taste of his hands
the smell of grief in the hollow sleeves
the sadness
his shoes

and they run to him laughing
as though he had been away
they dance at his feet as though
before a throne


## THE CURRENT


For a long time some of us
lie in the marshes like dark coats
forgetting that we are water

dust gathers all day on our closed lids
weeds grow up through us

but the eels keep trying to tell us
writing over and over in our mud
our heavenly names

and through us a thin cold current
never sleeps

its glassy feet move on until they find stones

then cloud fish call to it again
your heart is safe with us

bright fish flock to it again touch it
with their mouths say yes
have vanished

yes and black flukes wave to it
from the Lethe of the whales

## SOMETHING I'VE NOT DONE

Something I've not done
is following me
I haven't done it again and again
so it has many footsteps
like a drumstick that's grown old and never been used

In late afternoon I hear it come closer
at times it climbs out of a sea
onto my shoulders
and I shrug it off
losing one more chance

Every morning
it's drunk up part of my breath for the day
and knows which way
I'm going
and already it's not done there

But once more I say I'll lay hands on it
tomorrow
and add its footsteps to my heart
and its story to my regrets
and its silence to my compass

## TOOL

If it's invented it will be used

maybe not for some time

then all at once
a hammer rises from under a lid

and shakes off its cold family

its one truth is stirring in its head
order order saying

and a surprised nail leaps
into darkness
that a moment before had been nothing

waiting
for the law


BREAD

*for Wendell Berry*

Each face in the street is a slice of bread
wandering on
searching

somewhere in the light the true hunger
appears to be passing them by
they clutch

have they forgotten the pale caves
they dreamed of hiding in
their own caves
full of the waiting of their footprints
hung with the hollow marks of their groping
full of their sleep and their hiding

have they forgotten the ragged tunnels
they dreamed of following in out of the light
to hear step after step

the heart of bread
to be sustained by its dark breath
and emerge

to find themselves alone
before a wheat field
raising its radiance to the moon


HABITS


Even in the middle of the night
they go on handing me around
but it's dark and they drop more of me
and for longer

then they hang onto my memory
thinking it's theirs

even when I'm asleep they take
one or two of my eyes for their sockets
and they look around believing
that the place is home

when I wake and can feel the black lungs
flying deeper into the century
carrying me
even then they borrow
most of my tongues to tell me
that they're me
and they lend me most of my ears to hear them

## A DOOR

You walk on

carrying on your shoulders
a glass door
to some house that's not been found

there's no handle

you can't insure it
can't put it down

and you pray please let me not
fall please please let
me not drop
it

because you'd drown like water
in the pieces

so you walk on with your hands frozen
to your glass wings
in the wind
while down the door in time with your feet
skies are marching
like water down the inside of a bell

those skies are looking for you
they've left everything
they want you to remember them

they want to write some last phrase
on you
you
but they keep washing off

they need your ears
you can't hear them

they need your eyes
but you can't look up
now

they need your feet oh
they need your feet
to go on

they send out their dark birds for you
each one the last
like shadows of doors calling calling
sailing
the other way

so it sounds like good-bye


A DOOR


Do you remember how I beat on the door
kicked the door
as though I or the door were a bad thing
later it opened
I went in
nothing
starlight
snowing

an empty throne
snow swirling on the floor
around the feet

and on an instrument
we had been trying
to speak to each other
on which we had been trying to speak
to each other for long
for time
pieces lying apart there
giving off
echoes of words our last words *implor*
     *ing*
     *implor*
     *ing*
by deaf starlight for a moment

and you know we
have danced in such a room
I came in late and you
were far from the door
and I had to dance with
not you after not you before
I could reach you
but this was later than anyone
could have thought

thin
snow falling
in an empty bell
lighting that chair

could I turn at all

now should I kneel

and no door anywhere

# A DOOR

This is a place where a door might be
here where I am standing
in the light outside all of the walls

there would be a shadow here
all day long
and a door into it
where now there is me

and somebody would come and knock
on this air
long after I have gone
and there in front of me a life
would open


# A DOOR

What is dying all over the world
is a door

you will say That
is a dead thing

and you will be talking about the entry
to a chamber of your heart

you will say of that door
It is a thing

and you will be speaking of your heart

the streets will run over the wells
the wires will cover the sky
the lines will cross out the eyes
singing numbers numbers
numbers
numbers of
shadows of generations of armies with flags
the streets will run over the ears
trucks will run over the streets
no crying will be heard
nor any calling
the function of laughing neither remembered
so a tick coming over us
for no cause we by then
recognize
meanwhile in each cell the noise
turning higher as it
turns higher as it approaches
and still someone touching
a silence
an opening
may hear all around us the endless home


SURF-CASTING


It has to be the end of the day
the hour of one star
the beach has to be a naked slab

and you have to have practised a long time
with the last moments of fish
sending them to look for the middle of the sea
until your fingers
can play back whole voyages

then you send out one
of your toes for bait
hoping it's the right evening

you have ten chances

the moon rises from the surf
your hands listen
if only the great Foot is running

if only it will strike
and you can bring it to shore

in two strides it will take you
to the emperor's palace
stamp stamp the gates will open
he will present you with half of his kingdom
and his only daughter

and the next night you will come back
to fish for the Hand


AT THE SAME TIME


While we talk
thousands of languages are listening
saying nothing

while we close a door
flocks of birds are flying through winters
of endless light

while we sign our names
more of us
lets go

and will never answer



THE WHARF

*for Richard Howard*

From dates we can never count
our graves
cast off
our black boats our deep
hulls put out
without us

again and again we run
down onto the wharf named
for us
bringing both hands both eyes
our tongues our
breath
and the harbor is empty

but our gravestones are blowing
like clouds backward
through time to find us
they sail over us through us
back to lives that waited
for us

and we never knew

# BEGGARS AND KINGS

In the evening
all the hours that weren't used
are emptied out
and the beggars are waiting to gather them up
to open them
to find the sun in each one
and teach it its beggar's name
and sing to it *It is well*
through the night

but each of us
has his own kingdom of pains
and has not yet found them all
and is sailing in search of them day and night
infallible undisputed unresting
filled with a dumb use
and its time
like a finger in a world without hands


# THE UNWRITTEN

Inside this pencil
crouch words that have never been written
never been spoken
never been taught

they're hiding

they're awake in there
dark in the dark
hearing us
but they won't come out

not for love not for time not for fire

even when the dark has worn away
they'll still be there
hiding in the air
multitudes in days to come may walk through them
breathe them
be none the wiser

what script can it be
that they won't unroll
in what language
would I recognize it
would I be able to follow it
to make out the real names
of everything

maybe there aren't
many
it could be that there's only one word
and it's all we need
it's here in this pencil

every pencil in the world
is like this


SPRING


The glass stems of the clouds are breaking
the gray flowers are caught up
and carried in silence to their invisible mountain
a hair of music is flying
over the line of cold lakes
from which our eyes were made
everything in the world has been lost and lost

but soon we will find it again
and understand what it told us when we loved it


## THE PLACE OF BACKS


When what has helped us has helped us enough
it moves off and sits down
not looking our way

after that every time we call it
it takes away one of the answers it had given us

it sits laughing among its friends with wrong names
all of them nodding yes

if we stay there
they make fun of us
as we grow smaller because of the melting of our bones


## DIVISION


People are divided
because the finger god
named One
was lonely
so he made for himself a brother like him

named Other One

then they were both lonely

so each made for himself four others
all twins

then they were afraid
that they would lose each other
and be lonely

so they made for themselves two hands
to hold them together

but the hands drifted apart

so they made for the hands two arms

they said Between two arms
there is always a heart

and the heart will be for us all

but the heart between them
beat two ways
already for whoever
was to come

for whoever would
come after

one by one


## A PURGATORY


Once more the hills
are made of remembered darkness torn off
and the eye rises from its grave
upon its old
upon its ancient life

but at a wrong moment

once more the eye
reveals the empty river
feathers on all the paths
the despairing fields
the house in which every word
faces a wall

and once more it climbs
trying to cast again
the light in which that landscape
was a prospect of heaven

everywhere
the vision has just passed out of sight
like the shadows sinking
into the waking stones
each shadow with a dream in its arms
each shadow with the same
dream in its arms

and the eye must burn again and again
through each of its lost moments
until it sees

THE CHASE

On the first day of Ruin
a crack appears running

then what do they know to do
they shout Thief Thief
and run after

like cracks converging across a wall

they strike at it
they pick it up by tails
they throw pieces into the air
where the pieces join hands
join feet run on

through the first day

while the wren sings and sings


A  WOOD

*for Mark and Jill Sainsbury*

I have stood among ghosts of those who will never be
because of me
the oaks were darkening
we all knew who was there
sailing walking sitting as stones
ancestors ancestors I turned to say
always was it this way
from you did my shoulders learn
not to fly
my hands not to walk
my bones not to stay
from your blackbirds again and again
did I learn at evening
not to call myself home

## NOMAD SONGS

If I don't go there
nobody's there

———————

Every word
runs the hills at night

———————

Smoke
remember who let you go

———————

Ho it's spring
see
the echoes flying

———————

Birch tree with one arm
groping in death
hold onto it

———————

My cradle
was a shoe

———————

We leave a child
outside
as bait for the guides


## THE DIGGERS

If a man with a shovel came down the road

if two men
with shovels came down the road
if eight men with shovels
came down the road

if seventeen men with shovels came down the road
and I wanted to hide
I would see then that everything here
is transparent

yes that is what I would see but I would feel myself
then like my hand in front of my eyes
like this hand just as it is
in front of my eyes

and I would try to take it down
before they saw through it and found me


ASH


The church in the forest
was built of wood

the faithful carved their names by the doors
same names as ours

soldiers burned it down

the next church where the first had stood
was built of wood

with charcoal floors
names were written in black by the doors
same names as ours

soldiers burned it down

we have a church where the others stood
it's made of ash

no roof no doors

nothing on earth
says it's ours


## ANIMALS FROM MOUNTAINS


When I was small and stayed quiet
some animals came
new ones each time
and waited there near me
and all night they were eating the black

they knew me they knew me
nobody saw them
I watched how they watched me
they waited right there
nobody heard them talking laughing
laughing
Laugh they told me nobody will hear

and we went out one time
onto one mountain
all the way and nobody knew we went
we went together we sounded like chewing
the next day the mountain was gone

we went out onto two mountains
we made no noise
no more noise than smoke
nobody saw us far away
the next day those mountains were almost gone

we went out
onto my dead grandmother's mountain

there an old wind lives
that's never been away
it lives on and on there alone
but the mountain's gone
and some of us
never came back all the way


SIBYL


Your whole age sits between what you hear
and what you write

when you think you're getting younger
it's the voice coming closer
but only to you

so much of your words
is the words
once they've come out of the ground
and you've written them down
on petals
if it's spring

the same wind that tells you everything at once
unstitches your memory
you try to write faster than the thread is pulled
you write straight onto the air
if it's summer

with your empty needle

straight onto a face if there's light enough
straight onto hands
if it's autumn

## WHO IT IS

On the upper slope
the moon
smokes through the woods
someone is running there
silently waving
someone's father
not my father
no and not his father the drunk
no and not his
father the one that was murdered
no it is the first one
I don't know
it is his father
it is everyone I don't know
it is his father

why
is he running there

why is he running on the mountain

why is he waving why do I
not hear him
why do I not know him
why do I not know him why are they there

everywhere they have seen
their moon rising

MIST

Today seventy tongues
are hiding in the trees

their voices are hanging beyond the mist
seventy long banners mingling
red yellow
blue voices
hanging silent

here the nuthatch blows his horn
leading a thin procession of white wind

past the black trees
through the world


UNDER BLACK LEAVES

In one window
old moon swollen with our shadow
bringing it
to birth one more time

in another window
one of the stars that does not know it is the south
the birds' way

the mouse is no longer afraid of me
the moth that was clinging to my face
a day in some city
has been taken away
very old it clung there forgetting everything
nails have been drawn out of my ears

certain stars leaving their doorways
hoped to become crickets
those soon to fall even threw
dice for the months
remembering some promise

that game was long before men
but the sounds traveled slowly
only now a few
arrive in the black trees
on the first night of autumn


A SICKNESS AT THE EQUINOX


September yellows
a few of the wild laurels
from wet ditches still the loosestrife
as when I was born
and the days before

I sit in late sunlight hoping to be healed
shadows of leaves slip along me
crossing my face my chest
toward the east

to each of them
in turn I say Take
it with you

take with you leaf shape
little shadow
darkness of one leaf
where you are going

a brother or sister
you were afraid was lost for good

a mother a father
a lover
a child
from under there


## WANTING A SOUL IN THE SOUTH


The world is made of less and less
to walk out on farther
and farther
another year
is about to be taken away everywhere
someone still standing there
holding a basket

the planets glide doubting
among the bare rafters here
signaling
apparently
wrong wrong this house
moving out their year
all night the cocks crow
no

it's all right though
so far
walking on in the dark
over the breathing floors
through the rooms that are here
with my basket

HORSES

The silence of a place where there were once horses
is a mountain

and I have seen by lightning that every mountain
once fell from the air
ringing
like the chime of an iron shoe

high on the cloudy slope
riders who long ago abandoned sadness
leaving its rotting fences and its grapes to fall
have entered the pass
and are gazing into the next valley

I do not see them cross over

I see that I will be lying
in the lightning on an alp of death
and out of my eyes horsemen will be riding


SHIP

Far from here but still in sight

there is a fine white ship of everything we have loved
under full sail entering
among wrecks and many bridges
where birds are watching
always watching

same
birds with one wing

forgetters of singing

here it is they see coming to them again
from those who hate them


WORDS


When the pain of the world finds words
they sound like joy
and often we follow them
with our feet of earth
and learn them by heart
but when the joy of the world finds words
they are painful
and often we turn away
with our hands of water


ONE TIME

*for Charles Bell*

O venerable plank burning
and your pegs with you
the hordes of flame gaining
in the marks of the adze
each mark seven times older than I am
each furthermore shaped like a tongue
you that contain
of several lives now only a dust
inside the surfaces that were once cuts
but no memory no tree
even your sparks dust
toward the last some of your old pitch

boils up through you
many children running
into a shining forest


THE WAY AHEAD


A winter is to come
        when smaller creatures
        will hibernate inside the bones
        of larger creatures
        and we will be the largest of all
        and the smallest

A Monday is to come
        when some who had not known
        what hands were for
        will be lifted and shaken
        and broken and stroked and blessed
        and made

An eye is to come
        to what was never seen
        the beginning opening
        and beholding the end
        falling into it

A voice is to come
        that all the leaves
        wanted
        and the ears uncurled
        to reach for
        and one of them will hear it

Feet are already marching there
fields of green corn and black corn are already

throwing up their hands
all the weeds know and leap up from the ditches
every egg presses on toward those ends
for this the clouds sleep with the mountains

for this in the almanacs of the unborn
terrible flowers appear
one after the other
giving new light

A light is to come


SUMMITS


Mountains bloom in spring they shine in summer
they burn in autumn
but they belong to winter
every day we travel farther and at evening
we come to the same country
mountains are waiting but is it for us
all day the night was shining through them
and many of the birds were theirs


TO THE HAND


What the eye sees is a dream of sight
what it wakes to
is a dream of sight

and in the dream
for every real lock
there is only one real key

and it's in some other dream
now invisible

it's the key to the one real door
it opens the water and the sky both at once
it's already in the downward river
with my hand on it
my real hand

and I am saying to the hand
turn

open the river




FOLK ART


Sunday the fighting-cock
loses an eye
a red hand-print is plastered to its face
with a hole in it
and it sees what the palms see from the cross
one palm




THE SECOND TIME


The second time
the hills have shrunk
the bells are thinner
the hours have fewer colors
it seems that some of the old weather
must have been invented

the second time has white stone gateposts
at the head of a silent pass
under a pillar of sunlight
we see them only once
we see them only the second time
then we forget them

the second time has birds of its own
it has wings of its own
the second time comes with a picture

the second time comes with an old picture
of something not there
it clings to the picture
as to its life

death
begins the second time
with survival


EXERCISE


First forget what time it is
for an hour
do it regularly every day

then forget what day of the week it is
do this regularly for a week
then forget what country you are in
and practise doing it in company
for a week
then do them together
for a week
with as few breaks as possible

follow these by forgetting how to add
or to subtract
it makes no difference
you can change them around
after a week
both will help you later
to forget how to count

forget how to count
starting with your own age
starting with how to count backward
starting with even numbers
starting with Roman numerals
starting with fractions of Roman numerals
starting with the old calendar
going on to the old alphabet
going on to the alphabet
until everything is continuous again

go on to forgetting elements
starting with water
proceeding to earth
rising in fire

forget fire


## INSTRUCTIONS TO FOUR WALLS


Now one of you turn this way
just as you are
woman and girl all these years
speaking another language
as the earth does
and open your eyes
with the wall inside them

doubled
but going away
getting smaller and smaller
but don't you move
see how long it takes for me to appear there
and how old I am then
and how old I've been
if you can tell
but don't put on anything special for me
I want to see you as you are every day
as you see me
without my name

the one of you whose turn it is
to follow me like a dog
don't be the dog who's stolen something
don't be the dead dog
don't be the lost dog the sick dog
the watch dog
be the good brown dog that ran through both families
till you found me
be happy to see the back of my head
just where it is

and one of you be the sea
starting right there
older than words or water
opening into itself forward and backward
each wave lying still
with a piece of horizon in its arms
one sail going
one sail coming
two wings approaching each other

and one of you
stay still just as you are
with your door
be yesterday
be tomorrow
be today


IN THE LIFE OF DUST


Dust thrown into eyes
learns to see
and it follows

the first thing it sees
is a man holding dust in his hand
the next thing it sees is a hand scraping dust from the ground
the next thing it sees is the ground
and it rejoices

the next thing it sees
is footprints handprints in the ground
handprints long hollows
valleys in the earth
from scraping up dust

footprints running

the dust still feels them
remembers them coming
running
and now the dust can see

and it follows them
in its time it is everywhere
it is the dust in front of them

somewhere else waiting
watching

two men come running over the mountain
both of them blind

it sees that they are its children
and it beholds hatred
it beholds fear


## A FLEA'S CARRYING WORDS


A flea is carrying a bag of diseases
and he says as he goes
these I did not make myself
we don't all have the same gifts
beginning isn't everything
I don't even know who made them
I don't know who'll use them
I don't use them myself
I just do what's in front of me
as I'm supposed to
I carry them
nobody likes me
nobody wants to change places with me
but I don't mind
I get away
bag and all
something needs me
everything needs me
I need myself
and the fire is my father

# WHEN THE HORIZON IS GONE

When the horizon is gone
the body remains horizontal
the earth remains horizontal
but everything else
is vertical

the soles of the feet are vertical
so they can't climb
and they wait

the veins are vertical
so the blood can't flow
so it sinks
and there's no center to sink toward

what the hands hold is vertical
so they can't feel it
and they let go

what the eyes see is vertical
and always was
and they still don't recognize it

the sound is vertical
so they don't hear
anything

at first

calling

# THE LANTERN

A little way ahead
each is alone

when you see it you are there already
in one respect

for in that world nothing can break
so no one believes in the plural there
which is the first abstraction and the last
which is the and which is the between which is the among
so no one believes in us there
so at last there is only
the single
one
alone
held together by nothing
so the question of belief never arises

that is the place of a god
for a god is alone
he sits on each different leaf
he holds in each eye
differently
in each hand differently
one emblem of one aspect of his difference
each time it is single
each time it is an image of him
each time it is an image of you
each time it is an image of no one
carrying a lantern
each time it is different
from a different side
each time it is the same
well once you are there can you speak

if you were going to speak at last
which would you speak to

you open your one mouth
each image opens his mouth

you say nothing
once

you open a cave in the ground
one cave
each god closes each eye
you go down inside each eye
into each vein
into each vein of each leaf
into each root
no root has an eye
it has always been so dark there

but your eye is closed
so it's lighter for you

far away an empty lantern is swinging

image of no one carrying it

you start to follow it
to see his face


APPARITION


The more like a man it is
the more it frightens the birds
the more it frightens children
the more it frightens men

it comes wanting to live
but to live

it would have to fly up in itself
it would have to clap its hands when it could say nothing
it would have to tremble at itself


## A NUMBER


Those who come back from a number
are paler
they know that they're
one number the less
and whenever they talk
they talk about where they were
for each of their words has been there

and all the time they were gone
that number was here
not a day passed
without its turning up somewhere
well where then were those

who went out over unlit hills
bearing their words
to that number
and turned pale at what they saw
and keep talking about it

DOGS

Many times loneliness
is someone else
an absence
then when loneliness is no longer
someone else many times
it is someone else's dog
that you're keeping
then when the dog disappears
and the dog's absence
you are alone at last
and loneliness many times
is yourself
that absence
but at last it may be
that you are your own dog
hungry on the way
the one sound climbing a mountain
higher than time


THE WAR

There are statues moving into a war
as we move into a dream
we will never remember

they lived before us
but in the dream we may die

and each carrying
one wing as in life
we may go down all the steps of the heart

into swamp water
and draw our hands down after us
out of the names

and we may lose one by one our features
the stone may say good-bye to us
we may say good-bye to the stone
forever
and embark
like a left foot alone in the air
and hear at last voices like small bells
and be drawn ashore

and wake with the war going on

## THE WATER OF THE SUNS

In craters in the west other suns went down
and by morning no one believed it
no one has to believe it the mountains
aren't selling anything
some of the suns left gold
many left water for the next time

when you spend that gold you feel the night coming on
and nothing to make a fire
under all the empty mountains

but when you drink that water you begin to wait
you hear your time falling into you out of a stone
you begin to grope through your cold veins calling
like a bird before sunrise

till the morning that needs you

## A PRAYER OF THE EYES

There are stones here
that have to have been seen first
by a man many centuries old
who has gone into seven other worlds
and has come back without sleeping to look at these few stones
before going on

then the stones become visible to us as stones
but which ones are they
they are not marked in any way
those old men would not have
marked them in any way
those solitary men
why would they have wanted to mark them
after seven worlds
what mark would they have put
meaning what
on stones
that are never lost
and never anyone's

those men arrive
some of them in this lifetime
some of them only in this lifetime
sometimes somebody
sees them
may I see one of them
with his worlds behind him like wings
may I see the stones
as he sees them
may he show me the stones

# THE CRY

In many houses the cry has a window
and in one house the window is open

and the cry has flowed out like one drop of water
that once filled the whole room

there it is the first drop of water
from which everything came
when it is all over

a single drop of water is flowing
there on the white path into the hills

you would see it was a tear
because it is flowing upward
becoming a note in the still night

leaving its salt to the white path
that flows into the place far below
that once was sea

as you would know
if you were to stand in that doorway
if you were to open the door
if you were to find it

of the cry
that no longer sleeps there

so that if you were to see that window
from the outside
you would see nothing

## BY THE CLOUD PATH

No day has an age of its own
an entire year has no age of its own
    but there is a cloud in every picture

Those clouds are from almanacs not from calendars
    old almanacs
    taken from lovers given to prisoners
    given back
    found by children
    missing pages signed Cloud
    art is long
    a cloud is a monument to an eye

Know of the new buildings
    that some cannot be reflected in water
    all you will see reflected is clouds

    Who use those buildings sank long ago
    the question is can you still believe them

    their windows were calendars
    their moon was drawn in red
    but its heart was not there

The clouds dragging anchors are pilgrims
    the anchors are inside three sleeps
    in the prisoners
    in the lovers
    and in the children

From a window photographs of one face
    every day of its life

are reflected rapidly on a cloud
the sound is a recording of one tone
that face produced that day
of its own


A HOLLOW


Here then is where the wolf of summer lay
heard flocks of sheep running by
like rats' teeth on the paths
heard them in the stubble like rain
listened to them pissing from their thin bones
learned one by one the tone of each jaw
grinding its dry stalks knew every cough
and by the cough the throat

here lay with the roots around him
like veins around a heart
and was the wolf of summer
there were leaves that listened to him with their whole lives
and never felt the wind
while he lay there like darkness in an ear
and hearing notes of wells
knew where the moon was


FOR SAYING THAT IT WON'T MATTER


Bones of today I am going to leave you
where you never wanted to be
listen shall we talk of it now
I am going to leave you there
every bone that is left to itself

has been in trouble
it was born to go through it
every skin is born knowing that
and each eye

you are voyaging now through the half-light of my life
let us talk of this while the wind is kind
and the foam rustling on your bows
hear me I am going to leave you
on the empty shore
the sand will be blown away
we should talk about it
you were born for trouble
it is not for you that I am afraid
you will start singing camel songs

what can I say to you listen it is not for you
it won't matter to you
listen whatever you dream from then on
will be yours even if it was mine
unless it's me
listen you will still tell the fortunes of others
you will hang in the bell of earth at a wedding
you will fly on and on in white skins
by your own light


FOREWORD


We will tell no more than a little
about the first wing
the orphan

we will say nothing of his parents the giants
nor of the tree in which he was born

one autumn
nor of his sisters the grass
nor his brothers the fires

he was alone he was the first wing
it is all we need to know
everything here has two wings
except us

all we will tell
is how he found the other wing
his reflection groping downward through the air
and of the stream between them
where it rises
how flight began
why the moths
come and bathe in the dust
and it is a light to them


FINDING A TEACHER


In the woods I came on an old friend fishing
and I asked him a question
and he said Wait

fish were rising in the deep stream
but his line was not stirring
but I waited
it was a question about the sun

about my two eyes
my ears my mouth
my heart the earth with its four seasons
my feet where I was standing
where I was going

it slipped through my hands
as though it were water
into the river
it flowed under the trees
it sank under hulls far away
and was gone without me
then where I stood night fell

I no longer knew what to ask
I could tell that his line had no hook
I understood that I was to stay and eat with him


## THE PALACE

*for Harry Ford*

Music does not happen in a place
in it leaves do not grow
even if you try to put them there
there is nothing to see and nobody knows you
even if you were born there

yet the blood continues to follow music
the heart never sleeps urging the feet of the blood
to echo to rest nowhere
to pass near the skin to listen
whether music is anywhere
to look through a glass to go on
to go through
music never waits the heart says

the blood says nothing
the deaf queen pacing alone
through her thin palace
feeling music turning in the walls

# BALLADE OF SAYINGS

In spring if there are dogs they will bark
the sieves of the poor grow coarser
even in the dark we wake upward
each flower opens knowing the garden
water feels for water
the law has no face
nowhere are the martyrs more beautiful
the air is clear as though we should live forever

in summer if there are fleas there will be rejoicing
you kill the front of him I'll kill the back
every sieve knows a dance
each soldier is given a little bleached flag
ours are the only parents
the poor do not exist they are just the poor
the poor dream that their flowers are smaller
patience has the stones for a garden
the seer is buried at last in a gooseyard
the air is clear as though we should live forever

in autumn if there are trees eyes will open
one moment of freedom partakes of it all
those who will imitate will betray
the dogs are happy leading the archers
the hunter is hunted the dealer is dealt the listener is heard
the halls of government are the exhibition palaces of fear
anguish rusts
the poor believe that all is possible for others
each fruit hopes to give light
the air is clear as though we should live forever

in winter if there are feet bells will ring
snow falls in the bread of some and in the mouths of others
nobody listens to apologies
when prisoners clasp their hands a door locks

the days are polished with ashes
the cold lie in white tents hoarding sunrise
the poor we have with us always
the old vine stakes smell of the sea
the air is clear as though we should live forever

Prince it is said that night is one of the sieves
there is no end to how fine we shall be
at the names of the poor the eye of the needle echoes
the air is clear as though we should live forever


TO THE RAIN


You reach me out of the age of the air
clear
falling toward me
each one new
if any of you has a name
it is unknown

but waited for you here
that long
for you to fall through it knowing nothing

hem of the garment
do not wait
until I can love all that I am to know
for maybe that will never be

touch me this time
let me love what I cannot know
as the man born blind may love color
until all that he loves
fills him with color

## THE DREAMERS

In one of the dreams men tell how they woke
a man who can't read turned pages
until he came to one with his own story
it was air
and in the morning he began learning letters
starting with A is for apple
which seems wrong
he says the first letter seems wrong

a man with his eyes shut swam upward
through dark water and came to air
it was the horizon
he felt his way along it and it opened
and let the sun out so much for the sun
and in the morning he began groping for the horizon
like the hands of a clock
day and night

a man nothing but bones was singing
and one by one the notes opened
and rose in the air and were air
and he was each one
skin mouth ears feeling
feathers he keeps counting everything
aloud including himself
whatever he counts one is missing

I think I fell asleep on a doorstep
inside someone was coming
walking on white heads that were the best words I knew
and they woke at that step for the first time and were true
when I came to myself it was morning
I was at the foot of the air
in summer and I had this name
and my hand on a day of the world

## SEPTEMBER

By dawn the little owls
that chattered in the red moon
have turned into magpies in the ash trees
resting between journeys
dew stays in the grass until noon
every day the mist wanders higher
to look over the old hill
and never come back
month of eyes your paths see for themselves
you have put your hand
in my hand
the green in the leaves has darkened
and begun to drift
the ivy flowers have opened
on the weasel's wall
their bees have come to them
the spiders watch with their bellies
and along all the shores
boats of the spirit are burning
without sound without smoke without flame
unseen in the sunlight
of a day under its own king

## FLIES

On the day when the flies were made
death was a garden
already without walls
without apples
with nowhere to look back to
all that day the stars could be seen
black points

in the eyes of flies
and the only sound was the roar of the flies
until the sun went down

each day after that something else was made
and something else with no name
was a garden
which the flies never saw
what they saw was not there
with no end
no apples
ringed with black stars
that no one heard
and they flew in it happily all day
wearing mourning


## THE WRITING ON A FALLEN LEAF


The frost will come out under the stars
the falcons will grow thin as their voices
the fox will pretend to be old
the owl will bathe at night in the snow
the tracks of the hare will be empty shadows
I will forget


## SOUTH

*for Ralph Hilt*

To the south in the beginning of evening a dog
barks at his echo among mountains
beyond bare walnut trees tiles are still climbing old roofs
lines of women with long burdens the colors
of dried darkening blood

each line straight into mountains
colder already all north faces
turning into their shadows
beyond them sea
through day and night to the last white mountains
an end a wise man fire
other stars the left hand


## SPAN


I know hands that leapt from childhood to old age
youth was never for them however they held it
everything happened to them early or late
end of morning never found them
the entire day was a long evening
in August
they played no instrument for when would they have learned
if not in childhood
everything they did displayed impetuous prudence
and smelled of sand
they and their clumsy skills were their own age
with its two seasons


## MEETING


A thirst for meeting

A long line of ghosts waiting at a well
laughing
in the evening
and I am standing among them
the line runs through me

I feel it
a procession of dry clouds

let it be clear that there is no comfort in them
comfort is far away
that lay in ambush for joy
there is no fear in them they cannot hear me
there is only that thirst
the old cracked laughing

of dry leaves
shriveled trees broken stones
walls walls
and empty hands
held forward forever


HISTORY OF ALCHEMY


All the gold that exists was transmuted once
by men learning to change themselves
who broke it and buried it
those who found it
took it for a metal
wanted it for its own sake
to have rather than to foresee
and for them it was evil
and they declared that transmuting it was impossible
and evil

## THE INITIATE

At last a juggler is led out under the stars
tears begin to roll down his cheeks

he catches them
they fly through his hands

he sees the stars swimming up
in his tears
and he feels in his hands his tears
fly trembling through the night

what is that juggler singing
later when the morning star
is dry

he is singing Not a hair
of our head do we need to take with us
into the day

not even a hand do we need
to take with us
not even an eye
do we need to take with us
into the light

## THE SEARCH

When I look for you everything falls silent
a crowd seeing a ghost
it is true

yet I keep on trying to come toward you

looking for you
roads have been paved but many paths have gone
footprint by footprint
that led home to you
when roads already led nowhere

still I go on hoping
as I look for you
one heart walking in long dry grass
on a hill

around me birds vanish into the air
shadows flow into the ground

before me stones begin to go out like candles
guiding me


GLASS


One day you look at the mirror and it's open
and inside the place where the eyes were
is a long road gray as water
and on it someone is running away
a little figure in a long pale coat
and you can't move you can't call
it's too late for that
who was it you ask

then there are many of them
with their backs to you and their arms in the air
and no shadows
running away on the road gray as ice
with the leaves flying after them
and the birds in great flocks the dust
the stones the trees

all your terrors running away from you
too late
into a cloud

and you fall on your knees and try to call to them
far in the empty face


TRAVELING


One travels
to learn how not to look back
hearing the doors fall down the stairs
and the tongues like wet feathers in a high wind

only in the present are the voices
however far they travel
and fires raising hands between echoes

out of words one travels
but there are words along the road waiting
like parents' grandparents
we have heard of but never seen

each with its column of smoke
and its horizon beyond which nothing is known
and its sun


THE TRACK


To see that an ancestor has reappeared
as the print of a paw
in a worn brick
changes what you believe you are

and where you imagine you are going
before the clay sets

and what you think might follow you

over the floors
of the oven

the empty palace
with its many wings
its lighted stairs
its deep windows
its seasons
and its white sound
still soft underfoot

and when


PERIL


Where did you suppose the moths went
when you stopped seeing them

some that you've forgotten you ever saw
or never noticed
are standing in a circle
with their eyes inward

another joins them
coming from your window

the circle grows larger like a ring of dust
spreading on a lake of dust
it is that much harder for each of the eyes to see
in the middle of the circle the glass filament

born of a spider of air
on which is hanging and turning
the world where you are sitting
forgetting them
as the number rises
like the note of the thread

that has been too high for your ears
for a long time


THE SLEEPING MOUNTAIN


Under asters the color of my shadow
the mountain stirs in its cold sleep

dream clouds are passing through it
shaped like men lying down
with the memory of lights in them

wolf puppies from the cliffs
cry all night
when even the lakes are asleep

after the Ark was abandoned on the peak
stars appeared in it
and sailed off into the night with it

all at once it is nine years
on the plains of Troy
remembering the mountain asleep

on one wing like a human

GIFT


I have to trust what was given to me
if I am to trust anything
it led the stars over the shadowless mountain
what does it not remember in its night and silence
what does it not hope knowing itself no child of time

what did it not begin what will it not end
I have to hold it up in my hands as my ribs hold up my heart
I have to let it open its wings and fly among the gifts of the unknown
again in the mountain I have to turn
to the morning

I must be led by what was given to me
as streams are led by it
and braiding flights of birds
the gropings of veins the learning of plants
the thankful days
breath by breath

I call to it Nameless One O Invisible
Untouchable Free
I am nameless I am divided
I am invisible I am untouchable
and empty
nomad live with me
be my eyes
my tongue and my hands
my sleep and my rising
out of chaos
come and be given

# INDEX OF TITLES AND FIRST LINES

*Titles in roman, first lines in italic*